Advance Praise

"Motivation isn't a surface-level fix to be gained from an inspiring speaker or an incentive—it's the result of doing deeper things right. For organizations that want to get the best out of their employees, this book holds the keys to those deeper truths."

—DANIEL H. PINK, author of *When* and *Drive*

"John was a mentor of mine 15 years ago. His lessons then about leadership, and today in *The Motivation Trap*, will be key for any CEOs or leaders who want to grow their people and company."

—CAMERON HEROLD, founder of COO Alliance and author of *Double Double* and *Meetings Suck*

"I sat in a room of 50 entrepreneurs and watched with interest as John asked an audience member to stand in a red bucket. It was one of those moments when the anticipation in the room had everyone on alert. With some wizardry wave of his arms and a few direct requests, John shepherded that CEO into a moment of such acute clarity that she broke through years of not understanding exactly what motivated her in her business. Bravo, John, for putting some of your magic into a book for all of us."

—**CHRISTINA HARBRIDGE,** author of *Swayed*, and mischief executive officer of Allegory, Inc.

"As a physician, I've seen that true healing comes from within. Changing through motivation only burns us out and cannot bring actual healing. Similar to the body, an unhealthy organization requires a shift from within in order to heal and thrive. *The Motivation Trap* is a powerful tool for creating this internal healing within your organization."

—**KIM D'ERAMO,** mind-body specialist and author of *The MindBody Toolkit*

THE
MOTIVATION
TRAP

THE
MOTIVATION
TRAP

*Leadership Strategies
to Achieve
Sustained Success*

———

JOHN HITTLER

GREENLEAF
BOOK GROUP PRESS

This publication is designed to provide accurate and authoritative information in regard to the subject matter covered. It is sold with the understanding that the publisher and author are not engaged in rendering professional services. If legal advice or other expert assistance is required, the services of a competent professional should be sought.

Published by Greenleaf Book Group Press
Austin, Texas
www.gbgpress.com

Distributed by Greenleaf Book Group

For ordering information or special discounts for bulk purchases, please contact Greenleaf Book Group at PO Box 91869, Austin, TX 78709, 512.891.6100.

Design and composition by Greenleaf Book Group and Kim Lance
Cover credit: jar ©Thinkstock / iStock Collection / obewon and carrot ©Thinkstock / iStock Collection / akinshin
Cover design by Greenleaf Book Group and Kim Lance

Publisher's Cataloging-in-Publication data is available.

Print ISBN: 978-1-62634-539-3

eBook ISBN: 978-1-62634-540-9

Part of the Tree Neutral® program, which offsets the number of trees consumed in the production and printing of this book by taking proactive steps, such as planting trees in direct proportion to the number of trees used: www.treeneutral.com

TreeNeutral®

Printed in the United States of America on acid-free paper

18 19 20 21 22 23   10 9 8 7 6 5 4 3 2 1

First Edition

Table of Contents

Introduction

HOW IS IT that super-smart, talented people underachieve?

In my decades as a coach, working with hundreds of people, this question has always bothered me. Why are there so many people out there with the skills to succeed who are failing?

There's one counterintuitive reason that I see over and over again: These underachievers are being motivated to produce results. This may sound fine, but motivation equals a carrot-and-stick approach. This is the push-theory tactic. When pushed, human beings generally push back. When led effectively, human beings tend to follow willingly.

This book poses a simple question: Is motivation the most appropriate tool for accomplishing what you want?

More often than not, it isn't. In fact, I would argue that motivation rarely fulfills its purpose: to obtain effective, positive, passion-inspiring results from competent, high-quality human beings.

Motivation almost always involves some form of push, which is a forceful approach. I suggest here a shift from a forceful approach to a powerful approach. Consider how your team might react to being inspired by a united cause rather than pushed by the need to produce. Inspiration lives in the realm of power. In the end, force generates resistance, but power is infectious.

Whether you're trying to motivate your sales team to hit their highest revenue target ever or get your fourteen-year-old to clean his room and complete his homework, *The Motivation Trap* answers questions and concerns about why motivating people tends to be, in large part, a waste of time. We'll get into the statistics of how effective the outcomes of motivational events really are, why motivation consistently falls way short of expectations, and how to utilize simpler, easier, and trainable tools to engage people and help them learn, grow, strive, and transform. You will end up becoming a much more effective and capable leader, and your team members will love working for you instead of feeling pushed (read: motivated) by you all the time.

Having spent fifteen years coaching both high-performance teams and those striving for higher performance, I know from experience that motivation gets inserted as a default tool to accomplish many tasks, most of which would succeed much better (and with better attitudes of the people you are leading and managing) if motivation was not engaged. Team leaders have been trained (or fooled) to think that their job is to motivate, and so they engage an overused tool instead of a more effective one. It's that simple. They push rather than lead.

CEOs and team leaders from Fortune 500 companies and venture-backed start-ups often complain that they have trouble keeping their team motivated. What if it was not their job to motivate their team? What if team members were responsible for motivating themselves and bringing their own professional, positive, helpful, best selves to work each day? What might change with this expectation?

The challenge is not for CEOs to motivate their teams better. The real challenge is to recognize that motivation almost always shows up as the least effective tool to get the job done. If the sales team wants to hit their highest revenue target ever, you or I can most likely list several tools that might help leaders accomplish that worthwhile goal. Here are a few: training, new habits, collaboration, mentorship, coaching, technology upgrades (for example, better sales software), and creating individual and team purpose behind achieving the never-before-accomplished sales goal. Use of any of these tools will produce a better result for each team member; for you, the team leader; and for the organization you all work for.

In *The Motivation Trap* we will unwrap the energetic underpinnings of motivation, explain why motivation holds big limitations, and point out where and when to employ it as an effective tool in leading and managing teams. There really are great uses for motivation, but they may not be how you have envisioned them.

Then we will walk through alternative tools, explaining how your brain and your biology interact well with them. No tool is ever right for all tasks, and usually a combination of multiple tools works most effectively in creating big results for you and your team—or for you and your fourteen-year-old homework procrastinator! I will offer real examples from teams at both small and large companies to demonstrate the points as well as to illustrate both effective and ineffective actions taken by leaders.

Finally, I will offer several more effective tools and suggest how and when to use them to create high-achieving teams that find enjoyment in their work and employees who take initiative. Not surprisingly, these benefits tend to come about when you avoid overusing motivation in managing and leading people. Motivation, like salt in cooking, should be used sparingly.

In outlining and recommending more appropriate tools, I will often suggest combinations of tools that are both simple to employ and completely catalytic in their ability to create the leveraged results you and your team want. These combinations of tools will be suggested in a chronology that makes the sum of the tools much greater than their individual parts.

Who does not like simpler, easier-to-use tools that bring team members together to accomplish highly leveraged success?

If you're like most team leaders, this goal is the cornerstone of your role on the team—to produce great results for your team members, for yourself, and for your organization.

The most productive organizations I coach utilize tools that work in simple coordination with how our brains and biology function naturally. Working together with more than 100 companies over the last nine years, we have learned how to get the most from people by making sure that they run toward what they want to achieve—both in their personal and professional pursuits—as opposed to running away from a negative consequence or a punishment for not achieving what they want.

What would your team look like, and what would your company culture feel like, if every day all your team members ran toward what they wanted to achieve—on purpose, focused, and ready to accept and conquer challenges as one of the most fun parts of their job? I trust you might become a big fan of less motivation as well.

I wrote this book for a couple of reasons: to help people get what they want, to help people live their purpose and what I call their Genius, and to allow individuals and teams to enjoy their daily work.

It seems like a simple but powerful calling to unleash the individual and collective power of people to create big results. My life's purpose—my Why—fits this perfectly: I believe strongly that when we play boldly together, everyone wins BIG!

I invite you to become a fan of less motivation and connect instead with a more powerful set of higher-leveraged tools that produce much more predictable and satisfying results. Your teammates will love you much more as the leader, and your fourteen-year-old will begin to complete his homework without you having to prod him. Now, that's reason enough to invest your time in reading *The Motivation Trap*.

———

CHAPTER 1

Is Motivation the Correct Vehicle?

YOU'VE EXPERIENCED IT. Perhaps you sat next to me at a two- or three-day motivational seminar designed to sharpen our focus and resolve. The speakers were highly enthusiastic. The message was supercharged and really got the audience excited. By the end, every person on the team was completely jacked up to produce its best results ever. We all walked out on a high note, believing we would now be completely unstoppable in attaining our sales goals, team goals, and team culture.

Back at the office after the conference, you have customer service issues, your budget is frozen, and one of your top producers has been lured away to your biggest competitor. How does your motivation feel now? Likely pretty absent, if you tell the truth.

Motivational seminars, MLM participants, and financial advisors starting out all share one thing in common: They start with big motivation . . . and very predictably fail! My own financial advisor tells me that less than five advisors out of a hundred remain in the industry after five years, and 50 percent are washed out after less than 90 days! Why? Not because they are not the best and brightest. Not because they don't "really want it." They fail because they use less than useful tools (it just does not pay for companies to invest *anything* in the first 180 days) and then have to rely on "staying motivated" when they essentially have no other tools. Once the financial firm (or the network/MLM marketer or the motivational speaker) gets the tough ones who are willing to press on despite overwhelmingly poor odds of success, the "house" then sells to these people— training, support, seminars, and so on.

As much as the speakers can be entertaining, emotional, and good at spinning great motivational tales, their effect has a motivational half-life measured in hours—not even days. When that effect meets up with life's simplest challenges, that half-life can become even shorter.

That's why I have never been a fan of motivation. In short, it just does not work for the overwhelming majority of people subjected to it. In *The Motivation Trap* I will peel back the layers of this trend to "motivate the team" and then dig into why that move is both exhausting and ineffective. I'll outline the way our brains interact (poorly) with motivational techniques, the energetic effect of motivation on those whom you lead and manage—whether team members or family members—and then offer much more constructive tools to accomplish what you are most likely after in the first place—a positive culture in your team and highly leveraged results.

Motivation will most likely not help you achieve these goals, despite what you might have been taught and what the speakers proposed.

ARE YOU ENGAGING POWER OR FORCE?

Is there a big difference between power and force? Yes, indeed. Force equals an exercise in a necessary amount of dominance in order to create a result. In contrast, power equals a position, stance, or move that generates no counter. Knowing whether you are engaging in a forceful move or a powerful move can make all the difference, especially in the field of motivation.

For the most part, motivation is a well-meaning exercise in manipulation—a tit-for-tat or carrot-and-stick approach. There's nothing wrong with this approach, but it does have limitations. Consider a positively appropriate form of gentle, supportive motivation using a classic tit-for-tat approach. It might go something like this: "Let's get this project done today, and I'll treat the team to the first round of beers."

This motivation technique is culturally uplifting, spurs excitement, and drives activity—all in pursuit of a desired outcome. In this case, two outcomes will occur: the completion of the work today instead of some later date and a seemingly enjoyable celebration with the team after work. What's not to like?

To start with, this approach can and probably will work well—but not repeatedly. Because it uses effective, ethical, and well-intended manipulation, the next time this approach gets implemented, it will build on the quality of the previous occurrence. If the last outing with the team was great, the reward approach of drinks after work will be accepted longer than if the time with the team was mediocre or fell flat. At that point, the manipulation would backfire.

Manipulation—and therefore, motivation—consists of a forceful approach to create a result with a team member or a group of team members. Do you really want to engage in a necessary amount of dominance to manage or drive effective results? Do you want your reputation to be connected to driving people to produce unhappy team members rather than long-term team players whom you would hire again and again?

Perhaps, like me, you had an early boss or mentor who pushed you hard—certainly harder than you would have chosen—to get you to a level that you might not have seen in yourself. (I had two!) You may be very thankful for that boss or mentor. At the time, if you're like me, there were plenty of moments when you cursed or regretted that this person was in your life, at least for a short time. With the wisdom of hindsight, I am much more grateful for what I learned and who I became under their tutelage. Importantly, I have also noticed that the two people in my life who fit that category never motivated me or attempted to motivate me. They challenged, implored, and taught, but they never issued rewards for progress. The rewards that they and I both received showed up in my increased level of competence and confidence—rewards for which I am still grateful.

Was there a similar figure in your professional life? Were you grateful for his or her wisdom or ability to motivate? Most teachers, mentors, and coaches can motivate, and I suggest that they bring an even greater gift. A great teacher, mentor, or guide allows you to choose your path, and when you are doing the choosing, motivation is not needed so much.

I suggest that people choose motivation as a path of least (or lesser) resistance rather than deploying more powerful tools. Force is usually much simpler to employ than power, and, hence, manipulation and tit-for-tat deals often follow. Motivation comes quickly and easily, as opposed to a tool that might take more time, talent, or wisdom to utilize. Most tools that fit that latter description fall into the category I would classify as powerful. Remember, power equals a position, stance, or move that generates no counter.

Force always has to be justified. Power simply appeals to our humanity, that within us that uplifts, progresses, and could be classified as noble. Force moves us, at times against our will. Power invites us to move forward of our own choosing.

Now that you have a better understanding of the difference between force and power, let me ask you again: Are you engaging in force or power in your leadership role and in your roles as a parent, spouse, partner, and friend? If you answer truthfully, you'll begin to unlock the shortfalls and limitations, both high and low, of most human dynamics.

Consider for a moment your role as a friend or spouse. If force constitutes the normal operating mode, your relationship will take on the attributes associated with force. Perhaps you will want to control, dominate, or be right in a majority of instances. All three are classic attributes classified as forceful behaviors. You might also engage in comparisons, barters, and veiled requests. They often sound something like this: "I've done the dishes three nights in a row, so it's your turn tonight." This would constitute a veiled request, namely, "Please take responsibility for getting the dishes done tonight."

If you want to upgrade your leadership and management style, consider a simple, powerful shift from tactics and language that are forceful to tactics and language that are powerful.

YOUR BRAIN AND MOTIVATION

While you're motivating the troops, what and how does your brain engage in the language, emotion, and tactics associated with traditional motivation? More specifically, how is what you say and do received or interpreted by those whom you are supposed to be leading, managing, and motivating?

Our brains simply stop hearing repeated attempts at tit-for-tat motivation quite quickly. We can acknowledge what is said and still not "hear" the information very well. The limbic brain, the part of our brain that makes most decisions, is neither logical nor linguistic. Every emotion you experience resides here. Emotion drives decision-making, so it figures that most decisions are made from a sense of innate knowing and feeling rather than from a data-driven approach.

Humans use the neocortical part of the brain, which specializes in language, analytical thought, and logic, to justify emotional decisions we have already made. We make the emotional decision and then immediately switch to the justification, hence moving from the limbic part of the brain to the neocortex so quickly that we hardly begin to break down the actual process. It just happens.

Put all this together, and your attempts at repeatedly motivating people through an emotional approach that consists of "if you do this, then you get that" will work for only a short period of time before the reward has to increase in a rapid disproportion to the task to be done. The prize for the top seller or the reward for the favorite design just got much more expensive.

This tit-for-tat bargaining makes getting results using motivation an exercise in rapidly diminishing returns or, in the case where an organization invests in a three-day off-site kickoff campaign and pays for the speakers, the hotels, the travel expenses for the team, and the facilitators who run the off-site, a fairly unfulfilling return on investment. If it is meant to fire up the troops, chances are it will fall well short of expectations.

WHAT'S IN YOUR TOOLBOX?

Every carpenter or tradesperson works with various tools—different ones for different jobs. Some are super-specialized tools that are not used very often, and some, like screwdrivers and hammers, are used almost every day.

Is your managerial toolbox filled with the right tools for the job—the job of creating, nurturing, and enhancing a productive, positive team culture where people can do the best work of their lives? If the answer is not clear, chances are you could be using a screwdriver to cut down a tree. A screwdriver is a great tool, but it's not great for that purpose. Where does motivation fall in your toolbox? Is it the equivalent of your screwdriver or hammer and used every day for all kinds of tasks, or is it used sparingly?

I suggest that using high-quality tools, as any tradesperson can attest, will yield even higher-quality results in the direction you want to move—toward a work culture where your team members do the best work of their lives. If that is the case, what components need to be in place? Consider some of these possibilities: a safe work environment free from sarcasm or factions, suitable or leading-edge technology, top-tier talent, ambition, leadership, and autonomy. The list can be endless, but let's just start with some of these elements.

In order to foster and grow the most productive elements of your team, do you have at your disposal the necessary, useful tools as a leader and manager of people?

Are you well trained in methods to lead? Inspire? Tell stories? Empathize? Train? Collaborate? Mediate? Serve? Again, the list can be endless, and in the final summation, some of these tools are purposely outsourced to Human Resources, outside consultants, or members of your own team. You specifically do not have to be fully capable of performing these roles in your team, but you had better be ready to implement or access any of these tools on very short notice.

Consider the list of proposed skills and talents you might want in your toolbox. Is the ability to motivate conspicuously missing? Clearly, this is not by chance. We want leading-edge, powerful tools. Motivation is not one of these tools.

ONE, TWO, THREE, MOTIVATION'S LESS A MYSTERY

Given the notion that you are looking to become your most powerful self and lead others in a way that develops your team members into powerful players as well, it's little wonder that motivation's role is a bit of a mystery in producing high-leverage results.

Clearly, motivation holds at its foundation a base in force rather than power, so right off the bat, the people subjected to motivational tactics will automatically provide resistance. Human beings naturally react to being pushed by pushing back. Force versus force. This is the main reason motivation does not work over long periods of time.

Second, our brain biology simply does not support the process of deciding to do (or not do) a task based on a carrot-and-stick reward system. The human brain is much better designed to appeal to our sense of highest values, community, and humanity, making motivation an ineffective choice to lead, manage, or drive high performance in individuals and teams.

Finally, as skilled tradespeople know, engaging the right tool for any specific job becomes critical in achieving the desired finished product. In the case of team dynamics, the finished product will require that all team members get better every day in their role, enjoy their work, and collaborate with their team-mates. Motivation does not appear high on the list of tools needed to accomplish these objectives.

———

CHAPTER 2

The Precursors Needed for Motivation to Work Well

IN CHAPTER 1, we looked at the idea of using the right tool for the right job. Perhaps the job is motivating. Perhaps the job is leading or inspiring or just making this quarter's goals. In the end, your role generally consists of effecting forward movement in a manner that allows your team members to enjoy their work every day, to like working with their teammates, and to get a sense of satisfaction out of the activities that you are all engaged in. If the teammates are terrific and the product stinks, it becomes pretty tough to stay interested in playing the game. If the technology or service absolutely qualifies as super cool and leading edge, but the culture of the team and organization is toxic, again, human beings will not play for long periods of time.

You have to pass both tests—people and product—to have any shot at winning in a team game. Additional attributes will help your ability to succeed, but to start, these two fundamental ingredients of good people and good product make the game at work worth playing.

People get motivated to do all kinds of things—from getting in shape or clearing out the storage unit to winning the quarterly sales contest at work. That necessary motivation can come from you, the team leader, or it can come from the intrinsic motivation of various members of your team. Either way, it will begin to spur action and advance progress.

Assuming you have the people and the product in place as prerequisites, what do all people (or teams of people) have in common before they get motivated to make a change? If you answered "frustration," give yourself a gold star or a happy face.

Why frustration? The answer is quite simple but not always obvious. Have you ever been really frustrated by a medical mystery or by the fact that you cannot find a decent hot beverage container that keeps your morning mocha at the right temperature for the full length of your commute?

In either case, that frustration, like an itch, either keeps itching or perturbs you to take action toward a better, more enjoyable, or less painful outcome. You push your doctor to find answers or you buy a better coffee container as the logical remedy for your frustration. In short, you get motivated to scratch the itch, or you live with the itch.

If no frustration exists, then no reason to get motivated to take different action exists. Frustration is the precursor, the first step, in getting motivated to change. You must have a frustration of some sort, which we will call tension. The tension could be a situation or something material, such as a substandard product, or a relationship issue—almost anything. Once the frustration or tension gets painful enough or annoying enough, your motivation (to shift) has the necessary component to manifest powerfully. Without it, change will not usually occur.

Let's also consider frustration without any commitment to change. For most of us, these types of frustrations can show up as complaints, stress, or annoying posts on social media. If you're like me, you avoid people who have lots to complain about with little commitment to change. I call them whiners. For many people, there is not much they can change, so venting scratches their proverbial itch.

Let's also consider that not all tensions require or deserve motivation to change. The fact that your weight rose ten pounds during your vacation may not motivate you or bother you enough to do a whole lot. You may just need to get back into the normal workout routine and standard diet that you strayed from while on a holiday break. No need for venting, and no real motivation to make (large) changes due to a holiday excess of caloric intake.

If you and I had to get motivated to change every tension that arose in life, we would do nothing else. We use discernment to assess what justifies our higher effort versus an acceptance of circumstances that may not be entirely to our liking. When a tension arises large enough to warrant a necessary or desired shift in behavior or attitude, we get motivated to do something differently. When a large enough tension arises within our team or our family but not so much in us, we are asked to get motivated on behalf of someone else's tension. Herein lies the challenge.

For example, your team leader sets up a team sprint or a big sales goal for the quarter—rah-rah, incentives, rewards, tracking results, the works. The challenge for the team leader will begin with the announcement of the big sales goal, and that team leader will need to get you and every other member of the team motivated to play a game that you did not invent or ask for. In fact, you and your teammates could most likely list all kinds of reasons why the timing is not ideal, the market is not quite right, and your team does not have the required resources to pull off such an ambitious goal. No matter. Goal set. Game on. Now, let's get motivated!

If tension or frustration is the precursor to implementing motivation successfully, what frustration did your team leader experience that dictated a much higher sales goal for this quarter? Greed? Ambition? Requirement from the higher-ups? Chances are the game of "let's have our biggest quarter ever" exists in the same way that of "let's get a perfect report card" does between parents and children. Team leaders almost always want the best sales quarter ever without necessarily getting full buy-in from those who are then charged with producing those sales. Parents often want better grades from children who are less than willing to do the extra work.

Regardless, you are now in the game of staying motivated for an entire quarter, with a tension or frustration not of your choosing. Welcome to your life.

Precursor 1 sounds like this: A frustration or tension is *required* for any form of motivation to be needed or utilized.

WE'VE ALL GOT TENSIONS. WHAT'S NEXT?

You've got plenty of tensions. I do too. I want to sell more, lower my cholesterol, eat more organic foods, and make sure my kids make healthy choices. The list of challenges and tensions seems endless.

Tensions can drive motivation at the beginning, and the

amount of motivation or change needed sits in direct proportion to the severity or size of the tension involved. Take, for example, something familiar to all of us: traffic.

Clearly, longer and longer commutes, high-occupancy vehicle lane violators, wasted time on the roads, road ragers, and the price these frustrations take on our bodies and mood really add up. The driving is not the tension. The unnecessary or wasted time in the car creates the actual tension.

However, the reason most of us do not find much motivation to try to change traffic congestion or commute time rests with the shared sense of resignation that very little can be done to change the situation. We could live in a community that has less traffic than the one we live in, move to a new residence closer to our workplace, ride a bike, or move our work closer to our home. All these options seem unrealistic or involve quite a high price to pay. Instead, most of us simply endure the shared tension we call commuting, confident that it will not only get worse but most likely get much, much worse over time.

Because we share this societal tension, it's as if we agree to suffer quietly and simply bear our tension together. A general tension does this to us—it creates complaining and resignation among its sufferers. We feel helpless to shift the tension and simply give up and accept it as the way it is.

In contrast, when fewer and fewer of our clothes fit, our energy level seems lower and lower, and the thought of wearing a bathing suit at the lake this summer makes us cringe, we have a specific and very personal tension. Enough with plus sizes and "more to love" characterizations of our body type. It's high time to get started on reclaiming our body.

The difference? My tension about my own body type exists as very specific to my life, even if the predicament seems rather common to many of us. I have full authority to change the look and feel of my body. Unlike with traffic, I might also feel much more empowered to do something about my own beach body. Maybe other beachgoers would appreciate my efforts this summer too.

My frustration with my lack of fitness grows to the point where the thought of a body shape (and weight) change—large or small—seems way more attractive than continuing on my current path. This begins the process of change, often kicked off by a bit of motivation—the amount needed being dictated by the size or severity of the specific personal tension.

Step one in this process is simple and powerful: Recognize and voice a specific tension. That tension should almost always be expressed in first-person language (that is, *I* or *we*). Instead of "my waistline has gotten too big," which implies that the waistline is the responsible party, something spoken in the first person can initiate motivation and action more effectively: "I have allowed myself to gain weight and become out of shape."

The language does not have to be derisive or insulting,

but it should be very specific to the tension felt. First-person language places the responsibility for change on only one person: me!

Step two follows quickly, again in the first person. State the new possibility or direction for change. Remember, the amount of motivation or change needed always works in direct proportion to the severity of the tension and the proposed direction for change. Most people would propose wording something like this: "I'm going to lose 20 pounds."

It's specific and personal. When you lose your car keys, you (really, your brain) become almost obsessed with finding them. Why? Because finding lost items—car keys or weight—makes sense to your brain. Ever notice that you must have "found" the fifteen pounds you lost before, only to lose and then find them again?

Try this specific remedy instead: "I will keep my body weight at _____!" Your brain understands a specific desired number to get to and maintain much better than an abstract number of pounds to lose (and then possibly find again). Chances are, with this specific, personal tension, combined with a specific, personal objective or goal, your ability to motivate and make progress greatly increases.

Here's the rub, and it's simple. Your newfound motivation rests as the *spark* to get you started in a new direction. That's what you wanted, right?

You needed a spark to get going, but which direction should you take now? What are the parameters? What can you expect from your newfound shift in attitude? The problem is that motivation is neither designed nor appropriate for any of these strategic and tactical questions. Motivation exists as short term in nature, emotionally based, and fairly unfocused, and it works best under those conditions.

Using motivation to drive a long-term project or goal exists as an exercise in continually exerting an externally driven force upon a person or the collective of people on your team in order to make progress. You would not finance a company using credit cards, much as you cannot progress continually using motivation. The desire and drive to move forward have to come from a more appropriate, sustainable tool.

Precursor 2 sounds like this: A tension needs to be *specific* and *personal* to provoke action or change. The more specific the better. The more personal the better. Without these two elements firmly in place, motivation fades and the intended results fail to materialize.

CHAPTER 3

Timing Is Everything

IF YOU NEED a specific and personal tension for motivation to stand any chance, then let's get specific and personal. Remember, the size or intensity of the tension runs in direct proportion to the amount of motivation needed to get started. The more specific your tension, the better. The more personal your tension, the better. Consider this articulation of a tension very commonly overheard: "I'm sick of being so out of shape! It's time to do something about it!" Every gym franchise thrives on this sort of declaration to start off the year. In your head, you say, "This will be the year I get into the best shape of my life." Then you join a local gym, sign up for BODYPUMP or spin classes, and you're off!

Notice the specific tension. Notice the personal nature of the tension. Both characteristics are clearly present. The articulation, however, is a bit general in nature. I have done this too—speaking a concern as if it equals a clear direction. Compare it with the specificity and personal nature of a different articulation for the same tension: "I'm sick of being so out of shape! It's time for me to lose 20 pounds and tone up. I'm joining a 30-day boot camp, starting on Monday morning."

Notice the difference in the specificity between essentially the same tensions. In the first example, clearly, motivation could show up and spark (remember, that is the role of motivation—a short-term, emotional spark or catalyst) forward movement in the right direction. In the second example, the articulation of the tension already leans toward a plan of action aimed at producing results. The path toward addressing the tension is already present. That path is not dictated by motivation. That clear path begins the journey toward the use of a far more effective tool to make progress. In this case, the tools are new habits and a strategy to employ, both of which are helpful in losing weight.

Which example would most likely produce more tangible and desirable results after 30 days? Clearly, quickly getting motivated to spark a move toward a strategic solution should garner better results than would a general statement of disgust. The first articulation only outlines and complains about a state of undesirable health. It sets no clear path or remedy. It's much harder to find motivation or any action plan for a complaint. It's much simpler and easier to find the initial spark (that is, motivation) and then hand off the sustained action plan to more effective tools for making consistent progress. Without this handoff, every day you would have to drum up the needed motivation to stay focused and committed to going to BODYPUMP or spin class.

Why is the possible motivation present in the first example likely a poor fit to produce an acceptable result in 30 days? It's simple. With a general statement of disgust, there exists insufficient energy (or motivation) to get you out of bed at 5:30 a.m., six days per week, to attend a boot camp at a local gym or park or get to BODYPUMP or spin classes on time. Weather, fatigue, soreness, apathy, or plain distaste for the process all stand as barriers and impediments that motivation cannot overcome.

But why? Isn't that the idea behind motivation, to get you going positively in the right direction?

Timing is everything. Motivation is meant to serve as a spark, a catalyst, a placeholder of sorts for a much more suitable tool to take over for the longer term. Ever seen a spark, even an ember, glow for a long time? Nope. Despite the vibrant color and heat, a spark or an ember is short lived. It can lead to fire but not by itself. A spark needs to attach, partner with, or hand off to a more sustainable source of fuel.

Consider the making of a campfire at an overnight outing with your kids. Everyone is looking forward to time around the campfire, and it's your job to get it started and sustained.

You start with some pine needles, and if you're really up for teaching the kids, you use flint and steel to create a spark that lands on the needles. That spark and the needles are akin to motivation. They get the fire started. But imagine trying to keep a campfire going only with pine needles!

Once those pine needles have smoked and then ignited, you need very small kindling (that is, a different tool) before you start to pile on small and then increasingly larger logs. You do not start your fire with big logs. You start with pine needles and a spark. Likewise, you do not start projects with a completed business plan. That comes much later.

A campfire will thrive with increasingly different types of fuel. Similarly, motivation must be handed off to a more effective tool for you to wake up at 5:30 a.m., a full 90 minutes earlier than your usual wake-up time, get out of bed, get dressed, and drag your bedhead and soreness to the boot camp. Every day that you count on motivation to get you out of bed is like flipping a coin—you have a 50-50 chance of getting to boot camp. Once you miss a couple of days, you will most likely quit altogether, perhaps with a story about injury, inconvenience, or your new plan to get motivated for another form of getting back into shape.

What, then, would be suitable substitutes for motivation— tools that will keep you on track much better? Well, enter Precursor 3: Motivation is designed for a very short duration only and must hand off to other tools or strategies designed to drive a project forward.

The longer and more often you rely on being motivated over and over again for the same project or outcome, the higher the chances of failure. Consider how many times you could guess between heads and tails in a row. Motivation fits the same dynamic. You can use motivation for a day, but it works a bit less effectively the second day, and the pattern continues for each successive day you count on motivation to move you forward. The half-life is very short, much like your pine needles in making a campfire.

The key here is to move from the spark to the tools better suited for producing results over time. Consider these possibilities: inspiration, habits, systems, processes, purpose, tactics, and strategies. There are others, of course, but these tools are all needed (often more than one at a time) to move projects and outcomes forward in a more predictably successful mode than would (daily) motivation of your team members.

It's amazing how often the leaders of organizations and teams classify as one of their top priorities "to motivate my team" or "to come up with new ways to motivate." I've seen this with leaders of Fortune 500 companies as well as start-ups.

Many parents have a similar approach with their children, for example, with homework. When parents attempt to "motivate" their kids to do homework, they quickly run out of ammunition, as the carrots and sticks quickly stop working. Here are a few examples of attempts to motivate:

- "You cannot watch TV until your math homework is done." (threat)

- "You have to get your spelling word flashcards completed before you go to dance/soccer practice." (threat)

- "You won't get a star on our board for today unless you complete your social studies homework." (bribery)

- "You can have ice cream only if you finish your social studies project." (carrot and stick)

The list is as endless as, it seems, the malaise and lack of enthusiasm for doing homework today, just like yesterday and the day before. As the homework "team leader," your daily attempts to motivate your kids to get their homework done usually start to fall apart in September, with eight long months of some version of negotiation or conflict attached to completing the job. In the end, the daily dance of coercing your kids to do homework results in increasingly poor quality of the work getting done and increasing tension between parent and child. It's no fun for either of you. Motivation is simply a poor choice of tools, much as a screwdriver is not so suitable for cutting down a large tree.

The children on your team at work are taller, yes, and respond similarly to doing their "homework." Attempting to motivate the large children on your team on a daily basis works as well as negotiating or bribing your school-aged children. Every human intuitively knows the game. Incentives and punishments work about equally effectively, which is to say, not so well at all.

If motivation were used only for a spark, what then would be the equivalent energetic handoff to engage the team or the school-aged student in driving their own results, free from carrot-and-stick deals? Let's look at a few options. I'll go into much more depth on several of these tools in later chapters.

COURAGE

Does your team need courage to better succeed? David showed tremendous courage in taking on the giant Goliath. My guess is that this type of courage is not often needed on your team. Courage comes in varying degrees. Most often, your team members do not have to take on giants in a battle of life and death. More often, they simply need to exercise willingness as a useful entry point into the courage game. What if your team were simply willing to make a plan of action, willing to try out a different direction or take the first step, or willing to partner with another new teammate or outside contributor? Results would follow, almost certainly, in the direction of forward progress. The model would look like this:

Amount of Willingness/Courage = Amount of Forward Progress
Amount of Forward Progress = Additional Courage to Take Further Steps

Truth is, willingness guarantees no successful results, but unwillingness almost surely dictates zero results. A willingness to try, to work hard (or harder), to play together on the same team, or to set an ambitious goal—all of these actions produce much higher results than motivation ever can or will. The end result shows up in the progress that your team starts to make, the fun or challenge that they create, and the confidence that grows from making incremental or exponential progress.

With children doing homework, the same principle applies. Do your children exercise any willingness to struggle through challenging math problems or tough spelling words? Are you willing to allow them to figure out the work on their own? The sooner you require a sense of courage—in the simple form of willingness—the sooner your children doing home-work and your children at the senior VP level will move away from short-term stimuli and move toward more sustainable tools to get things done.

INSPIRATION

"Nothing will work unless you do."

—MAYA ANGELOU

"If you are thinking of quitting,
connect with what inspired you to start."

—UNKNOWN

When humans are inspired, they need not have all the answers, resources, funds, or teammates in order to succeed. Consider the inspiration shown by a teammate raising a child with a disease like juvenile arthritis or juvenile diabetes. Parenting stands as a challenging enough job without the added stress of medications, doctor appointments, and the inevitable interruptions in daily life brought on by a sick child.

When that same teammate organizes a half-marathon group to raise funds for research, your initial decision to participate could be motivated by a willingness to help, but eventually your success rests more upon the inspiration found in your teammates, especially the parent of the afflicted child, the child in need, and perhaps your own healthy children. Whatever inspires you (and it can be multiple factors) drives you forward, especially when the inevitable challenges arise.

When you are clear about your inspiration, you dramatically increase the chances for a (more) successful outcome. When my son was in elementary school, another student had an incurable form of cancer. Kathy was a bubbly, energetic girl, always with a big smile and a bright outlook. As her disease progressed, she underwent chemotherapy and radiation treatments, and every bit of her long hair fell out. Many in Kathy's class, spurred on by an idea from one of the students, shaved their heads, boys and girls, in an act of solidarity, support, and appreciation for Kathy's courage. One of the parents had caps made that said "Kathy's Kids," and the class wore them proudly, whether they participated in the haircuts or not. When Kathy returned to school, she was buoyed by the great show of support, and the family really appreciated the inspirational act.

Grade schoolers intuitively knew it. You and I know it too: "Nothing will work unless you do." Kathy's classmates could not cure her, but they could encourage and walk alongside her. In turn, those same classmates received a tremendous gift of inspiration—the inspiration that led to courage to persevere, even in the face of mortality.

If grade schoolers can do this, who are you and I that we cannot?

HABITS

Consider again the idea that the day has come for you to fully reclaim the shape of your body, increase your daily energy, sleep better, and generally increase your vitality and well-being. Since your motivation can only take you so far, here's another possible tool to help with the job: habits. Social scientists suggest that as much as 40 percent of what we do every day is habitual—that is, we do not really think about it. We are less than fully conscious while achieving all kinds of things.

Take your morning routine. Do you always do the same thing, something like this: wake up to an alarm at the same time each day, hit the snooze button once (or sometimes twice), eventually get out of bed, use the toilet, and then head straight to the kitchen to start the coffee? This all occurs in the first few minutes after you have gotten up, and the variance in the (habitual) routine rarely changes. You don't really think about what you are doing; you're effectively on autopilot.

When you leave the house, do you always lock the door with the same hand? When you get into your car, do you do so the same way?

I do too. We're habitual.

If you're really going to transform both the shape and the vitality of your body, why not put the power of habitual behavior to work to create what you want? Habit will serve you much better than motivation. When faced with making decisions, motivation is temporary and situational. For example, you may have to "get motivated" to drink only bottled water when the team goes out for drinks after work. You may have to "get motivated" to attend the 6 a.m. exercise class since no other time will work in your schedule.

Habits work more effectively than motivation for a couple of reasons. First and foremost, you create habits by design, and in most cases, you do not change them much. To the extent that you choose to design and implement new habits, you shift your outcomes. You develop repetition until not doing the activity would feel much weirder than actually doing it. Ask people who work out when they have to miss a week of training. They just do not feel quite right, as they are in the habit of moving four or five days each week.

Second, habits work because we become not fully conscious of the actions after a while to the extent that the actions move us in a direction we would like (for example, more strength, flexibility, energy, and muscle tone); then, consciously choosing and implementing those actions supports our chosen outcomes. Social scientists now believe that it takes between

67 and 200 days to fully enact a habit—much longer than commonly believed.[1]

Consider these two simple shifts in habits over the coming 66 days:

"I replace soda and alcoholic beverages with water."

"I wake up at 6 a.m. to work out for 60 minutes before going to work."

If you exercised just these two habits, regardless of whether you felt motivated, your body would change over a relatively short period of time. At that point, you would be more likely to adopt either habit permanently to support your ongoing health and vitality.

Try it and see. My guess is that you will like the feeling of energy and renewed health much more than you will the feeling of lethargy after eating poorly or having two rounds after work. Your success will fuel your ambition to create even more healthy habits. Just ask people who work out a lot and eat well to support their vitality.

Also, compare how much water you would drink and how many days you would exercise for 60 minutes at 6 a.m. based upon motivation. Habits stand as a more effective tool than does motivation when you're ready to change, redesign, or transform your most important outcomes.

---

1 Phillipa Lally, et al., "How Are Habits Formed: Modeling Habit Formation in the Real World," *European Journal of Social Psychology* 40(6), October 2016.

When team leaders (or parents) tell me that their number one role is to motivate their team members (or kids), I know that their team is most likely not performing at a high level. I also recognize that they are most likely very stressed or exhausted. Employees will bring their own motivation. Inspire your team. Implement new habits. Watch the outcomes come faster and easier. Chapter 8 contains a deeper discussion on effective habits.

SYSTEMS AND PROCESSES

When you and your team (or family) implement and follow agreed-upon systems and processes, many daily activities are simply executed much better. Take, for example, something as simple as cleaning up the dishes in the break room or the dishes from the dinner table. Is there a rotating schedule for who does the dishes? Are there agreed-upon standards for an acceptable level of "clean" among team or family members? Is the division of labor relatively equal and fair? When agreed-upon systems and processes exist, motivation is simply not needed or recommended. The systems and process carry the energy or action forward.

In the end, if the break room is clean at the end of each work day, do you really focus much on the level of motivation implemented by the person whose day it was to clean? Right. Neither do I. A clean break room trumps how someone might feel about their process for motivation to get that job done. One team member can groan about the "slobs" who wrecked the kitchen, and another team member can clean the same kitchen with his headphones on. Either way, as long as each team member follows the accepted system, the kitchen becomes much more functional for all to enjoy.

Systems and processes are simply not dependent on how motivated or "in the flow" you are, and they do keep many functions working really smoothly—at least much more smoothly than does motivation.

Again, is it simpler to teach a system or process or to motivate someone to clean the break room or the kitchen at your home?

As quickly as feasibly possible, try replacing motivation with a more effective tool. A sixteen-pound sledgehammer will not function so well to cut down a large tree. So, too, motivation will not function better than agreed-upon systems and processes.

———

CHAPTER 4

The Pilot Light That Rarely Goes Out

REMEMBER, WE ALREADY agreed that motivation works only for short periods of time. We had a sort of pinkie promise on that, so let's keep that in place—at least until the end of this chapter.

Motivation does have a terrific purpose. Really, it does but perhaps not in the manner that you might think. The trick is that motivation fades quite quickly for almost all humans. We are just not wired to jack ourselves up daily, weekly, monthly, or quarterly, despite what conferences, great speakers, and sales managers want us to believe. Every clichéd sports movie includes a motivational speech that propels the underdog team to the most unlikely of comebacks from nearly certain defeat. Not sure about you, but my life does not resemble a clichéd sports movie, and I would be willing to bet that your life does not follow that plot either. If your team leader, spouse, or best friend gave you a motivational pep talk every single day, how long would it take before you ran out of patience for the continual messages? How long before they each ran out of new material for their daily pep talks? You get started with motivation. You get results with additional, more effective tools.

The problem is, motivation works really, really well until the world conspires to interrupt that newfound stimulus, which is to say, motivation works anywhere from a couple of minutes to a couple of days, and then it must be replaced with a more effective tool or strategy designed to create more lasting behaviors. Motivation can fall flat quite quickly, much like attempting to keep a campfire going with pine needles or not sleeping much and using energy drinks to keep you going.

After the initial moment of motivation, what is the most powerful tool you could next employ to ensure best results? There are many you could choose, and I suggest a very powerful tool at this stage. We call it your Why.

WHY AND HIGHER PERFORMANCE

Mark Twain famously stated: "The two most important days in your life are the day you are born and the day you find out why." His point applies more than ever today. Consider two of the best days in the life of any of your teammates: the day they are hired to do a job and the day they know why.

Do your teammates have any idea of the purpose, or Why, behind what they do every day in the workplace? Take out the obvious (commercial) fact that they are earning money, and you as the team leader have to create a purpose or meaning larger than any one member of the team—the purpose behind *why* you do what you do.

I am fortunate to know my Why in life. My Why is to play boldly with others so that we can all win big. Nothing complicated. Let's play . . . boldly . . . together . . . and win big.

When asked to work with teams and individuals, I always ask myself, "Are they willing to play boldly . . . together . . . and win? Am I willing to play the same way?" As crazy as it may seem, many people are not willing to play this way, despite the obvious advantages. They are fine to choose another manner of engagement. I just know that when my purpose in life is not connected to their modus operandi, we will not produce very good results together. There is someone else for me to partner with and someone else for them to partner with.

Does every member of your team know the overall Why of your team? If yes, do they know their own personal Why? Does each teammate's Why align well with the team's Why? Most of the time, this alignment seems pretty seamless, as a team Why and a personal Why both exist in a positive aspirational tone and, as such, generally link well.

Consider the probable or even possible results in your team if you utilized daily motivation to energize and drive them, and compare that outcome with the results in your team if each teammate worked with the clear knowledge and understanding of the Why for the team, the project, and the teammate's own life. Purpose usually takes a bit more time to figure out in the beginning, but once in place, it provides the constant driver and focus for every team member, as well as for the team as a whole. I worked several years ago with Tech Rescue, an outsourced IT firm with more than 60 employees. It was the type of firm that small- and medium-sized businesses engaged to manage IT needs for a monthly fee. The firm was growing quite well, but its number one issue was employee retention. Right behind that were the complaints about the techies who showed up to do the actual work.

Consider a common scenario that this successful IT firm experienced all too frequently. An emergency call would come in from a client whose network and website had crashed, causing a temporary work shutdown. In short, a five-alarm business emergency that Tech Rescue was perfectly designed to solve. Woo-hoo!

A senior IT consultant from Tech Rescue would be dispatched, arrive promptly, and diagnose and fix the issue at the client's office. The client was usually back on track within an hour. What's not to like?

The complaint from clients was usually that the senior IT consultant did not seem to listen, treated the clients as if they were idiots, and simply fixed the issue without any passion or connection to the people or the firm involved.

The company founder wanted to motivate and train her employees to become better listeners, more empathetic, and friendlier with the clients. Our team suggested otherwise, since some of the techs repeatedly took great care of clients and received satisfactory and even exemplary reviews. Most of those techs also stayed on the job.

The founder insisted that her team had hired the best and brightest and had a bulletproof process that was instilled in the hiring process. Team members routinely trained and tested the techs to make sure that they were fully capable of handling the challenges when they arrived at a client's office.

The founder was really clear about her personal Why, or purpose: "I believe in making everything and every person better by my participation." To pull off a personal Why like that, you have to care at a very deep level—both for people and for results. The techs who were rated poorly rarely received that rating because of faulty technical ability. They received poor ratings because they seemed to dismiss the concerns of the clients and to focus solely on doing the work—ignoring perhaps the more important human issues such as instilling confidence, showing empathy, and, oh yes, exercising a high sense of caring. Essentially, the techs just wanted to do the work—uninterrupted by nontechnical people!

The simple but not so obvious solution boiled down to this: hiring only people who really cared about others. Caring tends to exist as an attribute or characteristic that people learn early in life and do not learn so well later. Tech Rescue was attempting to motivate and train people to care. How do you do that if the team members are not aligned with caring as one of their highest values? The founder was the type who knew every employee, most of the spouses, and the children of the spouses. This was not a tactic. She just cared about those in her tribe! Rather than attempting to motivate and train employees to care, we suggested that Tech Rescue start every interview asking the job candidate to tell them about their last great volunteer experience.

If the candidate looked at them oddly, the interview was essentially over, as the candidate's confusion confirmed that the candidate had never cared enough about anything or anyone to volunteer time and talent. If the candidate offered a great story about a volunteer experience, the follow-on question then came: "Was this experience from high school or college as a condition to graduate?" A yes answer clearly suggested that the candidate would only volunteer as a requirement, which also indicated a low level of caring for others.

Did these candidates really not care about others? No. They simply did not exercise *intentional care on purpose* as the founder did. They did not emulate the Highest Purpose, or Why, of the founder and the organization.

Tech Rescue implemented the simple question at the front of their hiring process, and within eight months, their client reviews had dramatically improved and their turnover had gone down to almost zero. The people entering the firm still had very high-caliber technical skills, but more importantly, they cared about people as much as the founder did. The organization and individual purpose were aligned! The company had to interview more candidates to find people who authentically cared about others, and quickly enough the hiring staff learned to conduct a "pre-interview" with the key filter question; as a result, they only invested time with candidates that they sensed fit their highest value. All the candidates still had the high technical abilities associated with the IT work, and now their cultural fit matched the DNA of the founder and the rest of the team.

The Why and, as we shall see, Highest Purpose solved an ongoing, costly problem that motivation simply could not. Like a pilot light that rarely goes out, purpose continues to burn steadfastly and constitutes a much more foundational tool than does motivation, since, as with the pilot light, changing circumstances do not turn purpose off.

The Power of Motivation Handing Off to Your Why

When you use motivation to spark your next immediate actions, progress gets off to a good start. When your initial motivation hands off to a more powerful tool—Highest Purpose, or Why—your intentions, design, and execution all partner in full coordination with your highest values, purpose, and sense of contribution to your life and to the lives of others. That power tends to withstand the challenges that will come your way, as you are directed by your highest values, beliefs, and directives.

What would your life or the life of your team look like if every decision, every action, and all relationships were tied to your Why? Would you work with the same teammates? Would you serve the same clients? Would you employ the same vendors? Would your team meetings take on different dynamics? Might you even switch vendors or clients who do not meet your Why?

I suggest that your team would look a whole lot different, and it would most likely function differently as well. First let's figure out exactly what you and your team stand for at your highest values, or at your foundation. Here's a simple way to engage your brain to know what you stand for most. Connect with the last time you were really angry—I mean livid—at a person, a situation, or a condition. If you do not have an episode that comes readily to mind, then connect with the biggest pet peeve that you hold.

Now tell the short story about the episode or pet peeve. Here's an example. I only get really upset when I see a parent, usually in a grocery store, physically "disciplining" a young child, usually in the cereal aisle, where the two-year-old is grabbing brightly colored cereal boxes. The parent usually warns, then quickly threatens, then hits the child. In my book, this is inexcusable, and it makes me really, really mad.

Normally, other shoppers in the vicinity avoid that aisle due to the commotion and crying involved. I do just the opposite. I purposely move down the aisle until I reach the parent and child and then gently ask, "Could I help?" This almost always heightens awareness for the parent, and my tone is designed to calm the child a bit. I do not leave until the safety of the child is secured. It's usually awkward for the parent involved, but my focus, of course, is on the child, not the parent.

So why is knowing my pet peeve important to knowing my highest values, and hence a good clue to my purpose? Easy. We only get really worked up about things that matter deeply to us. If treating people well did not matter to me, I would act as many others do and avoid that aisle until the commotion died down. To me, honoring people represents a highly held value, so I enter rather than exit the scene when a child, of all people, is not being treated well.

What really gets you worked up? Once you have the violation, see if you can name the super-high attribute that you hold so dear. That will most likely be one of your highest values, and your purpose will almost certainly be connected to that high value. You can do this for a team, for an organization, and as an individual. State this as a simple, powerful belief.

My Why goes like this. "I believe that when we play boldly together, everyone wins big!" It's not exactly tied to my violation (which is treating people poorly), but you get the idea. When I play boldly with people, I love that we both win big. The converse of this rests closely to my strong sense of violation when people treat each other poorly, violently, or disrespectfully.

When you work with a heightened state of purpose, or Why, your actions and drive carry a fuel that relaxes you at the same time as it drives progress forward. That intersection of beauty and power collide when you and your team work fully connected to your Why. Every teammate, every client, and every project then tends to fall in line with your highest values, beliefs, and objectives. The need to motivate fades quickly.

What's in the Why?

Consider what might happen in your team or family if you lived from a clearly articulated Why. By "clearly articulated," I mean that all voices contribute to discussions and decisions, and all voices are heard in the creation of the team's Why. Finding your individual or team Why takes effort and full intention. More on that in a later chapter. In the meantime, here are four suggested areas to review and make choices for yourself and with your coworkers as a team.

Friends and Family

One of the greatest barriers to high(er) performance shows up in the company that we keep. If you subscribe to Jim Rohn's theory that "we are the average of the five people we spend the most time with," then who among your "Top 5" needs to go? Your gut already knows that you hold on to one relationship (or perhaps two) with that person who holds you back or violates your Highest Purpose or your highest standards. Perhaps they envy your success or your goals, so they quietly sabotage your efforts. Perhaps they simply have little or no ambition. Do they employ a "batteries not included" approach to life, such that you or someone else has to supply all the energy in the relationship?

Regardless of the reason, are you ready to move closer to your Why by upgrading your "Top 5"? That might start by quietly exiting a relationship that sits in direct opposition to your Why. It's a tough move, and it's necessary if you are to enjoy the power and beauty contained in living according to your Why.

Team Members

If your business is growing, you cannot afford to have any team members who do not pull their weight and (even more importantly) do not show up with a positive attitude. Is there one person on your team right now who pulls everyone else down? Not only that, do you get the sense that the person knows that he is not cutting it in his role? Either way, whether the team member brings a poor attitude every day or simply cannot successfully fulfill his role, he impacts everyone who has to come in contact with his attitude or his substandard work.

Imagine the pressure on this team member if he carries the burden and stress of being the weakest link and perhaps the team's barrier to growth. How would you feel if this were you? My guess is that you would want out of the role and perhaps even out of the organization.

In the end, people can work almost anywhere. If they thrive, work looks and feels great. If they struggle, especially without a clear path toward individual success, work can become completely debilitating and extremely stressful. Why not make the most generous move you can and help this one person move on? Every member of your team will applaud the action, most notably the person who leaves. That person will be ready for the next great success and, once settled in a new opportunity, may even thank you for demonstrating the courage needed to help him find employment with a better talent and attitude match.

Vendors

Do you engage vendors who do not align with your Highest Purpose, or Why? I bet you might. This is the vendor who makes inappropriate comments to your staff or talks poorly about you or others when in your office.

Here's the real question: Would you have this person or the company she represents in your home if you were not there? If the answer is anything other than a resounding yes, most likely that vendor does not align well with your values or purpose and as such becomes a poor reflection of you to your team and to your clients. Your team will applaud upgrading this outsourced service to a better-fitting vendor. Hire another company that fits your values!

Clients

Every person on your team has that one client whom they dread dealing with. Perhaps the client treats the staff poorly or rudely. Perhaps she does not pay the invoice anywhere close to on time while insisting on special priority service. When the caller ID shows the client's name, everyone avoids picking up that line. When that one client enters your workplace, each teammate tenses up.

My guess is that you might not realize that your team struggles with specific clients, because the clients treat you differently than they treat the rest of the team. Here's how you find out.

Have a very short meeting and allow your team to "nominate" any three (or five) clients that really need to go. See how much agreement there is about the candidates. You possess one "veto" from the team's list but with this caveat: You agree to meet with the client you would like to keep and explain the house requirement to treat every member of your team well or get cut. My suggestion is to allow your team to have the meeting without you present so they can speak more freely about which clients make the list. If you want to test the power of this approach, ask them how many candidates it took to come up with the final list. I would be surprised if there was much dissension among the team—they know the clients who cause grief!

When you model the ethic that any one team member is more important than any client or customer, you send a very strong message to your team: You matter, and I stand behind the great work you do. Clients will pick up on this message as well, and they will respect your approach and treat you and your team well. When your employees love your company and the team they work with, they will in turn take great care of the clients. Give them the power to weed out the small number of clients who simply do not appreciate what you and your team does.

If this ethic is not embedded into your company culture or the articulation of your team's Highest Purpose, then it should be. It solves multiple issues for the team and greatly unites the team members in taking great care of your customers.

Align these four areas in your business with your Highest Purpose, or your team's Why, and watch what occurs. It will be far more powerful, sustainable, and exponential than anything motivation could ever achieve!

———

CHAPTER 5

Inspiration and Leadership Beat Motivation Every Time

A GIFTED COFOUNDER of a company I worked in many years ago bristled when I once asked him why we didn't motivate our team members to become the best people, employees, spouses, and friends they could possibly be. His response: "We're not motivating anyone. Motivating people constantly is completely exhausting!"

He was absolutely right. If I had to take responsibility every single day to motivate everyone who had a poor night's sleep, a lousy breakfast, or a bad weekend, all I would ever do would be motivating people. My cofounder asked me, "Is that what you want to do all day, become responsible for the motivation of others?" Again, he was spot-on. The last thing I wanted was to take on every situation where team members needed to be uplifted by some sort of short-term method or tool just to get them to do what it was they had already agreed to do and were paid to do. They were professionals, after all, and coming to work ready to go was an implicit part of the agreement we held with every team member.

Instead, claimed my friend, we would simply inspire and lead people to become their best and set up the culture of our company to become a "playground" (his word) where everyone could do the best work of their lives. The idea was simple and brilliant at the same time. Instead of enticing, inviting, and manipulating people to play full out, simply offer the room for them to create and produce in a manner they never had been allowed to before. Those who wanted to play would step up and thrive. Those who wanted to complain or stonewall would step out rather quickly. In the end, motivation exists as an external stimulus or push, and inspiration and leadership exist as an attraction pull. Those who want to play without having to be pushed play willingly. Those who cannot be led to greater success opt out.

That company produced both great results for our clients and a great working environment for our team members. Not surprisingly, it became a great place to work and a profitable venture, and we spent almost no time at all with contests or pushing people. We invited every member of our team to do the best work of their lives, and those who aspired to that played willingly and took great care of the clients.

The steps to produce that healthy and vibrant culture were surprisingly simple. First, we differentiated between inspiring and leading. We were strategic about when to employ an inspirational tool rather than a leadership platform and vice versa. Let's explore the differences here so that you can engage both of these powerful tools—inspiration and leadership—as well.

Note: At no point were we tempted to take on the exhausting role of chief motivators of team members. We had a successful company to run and simply had no time for that job.

INSPIRATION AS A POWERFUL TOOL

When do you inspire versus lead? What's the difference, and what outcomes occur when you engage one tool versus the other?

To start with, both the etymology and definition of the term *inspire* might help our cause. *Inspire* derives from a Greek term that literally means "to breathe into," as to breathe life into someone or something. Many definitions include the notion that a divine or supernatural nature provides the power behind inspiring someone. You may be familiar with the concept "breath of life," either from the first book of the Bible, where God created man, or from mysticism and games where slain creatures are revived. Inspiration holds that quality, without the religious or secular suggestions: When you inspire others, they feel revived and more energetically able to take action.

Consider things that inspire you or give you a sense of life or an uplift. Beauty—especially that found in nature, such as a powerful waterfall, a rainbow created from a storm, or a terrific sunset—inspires us artistically, romantically, and aesthetically. We feel full of life for having been in the presence of the beauty and power provided by nature. When you are in nature, any of these occurrences tend to put spring back into your hike or propel you forward.

The key here is that the "life" becomes internally focused or based rather than remaining an external stimulant or irritant. We own the life breathed into us, regardless of where it came from. When you as a team leader or as a parent "breathe life into" those on your team or in your care, you produce an outcome that requires much less maintenance than does motivation or any other less sustainable tool.

How can we "breathe life into" ourselves and others? How do we inspire ourselves and others? There are two primary ways to inspire individuals and teams naturally.

Believe in a Cause and Take Action

You may have been completely inspired by a family raising funds for a child with an incurable disease. We all have witnessed the power of both the family and the child taking decisive action and moving forward rather than focusing on the debilitation that the disease causes. This steadfast belief "breathes life into" our less dramatic goals to care for ourselves (like getting into better shape) or to care for others (like raising funds for the cause), and our newfound life becomes internal. By that I mean no one has to hound us about our newfound life force. We own it naturally and willingly.

Compare the natural sense of ownership associated with getting in shape by means of your own drive with that of getting in shape while raising funds for a cause that inspires you— for example, a walk or run to raise awareness and money for a cure. When you get in shape to look and feel better (without the added inspiration of a cause), the urge to cheat on the diet or skip a day of scheduled training becomes much greater.

Imagine the power of you and an entire team sharing the inspiration, or breath of life, associated with a product launch, a charitable endeavor organized at work, or the end-of-the-year office party. Might it make the outcome more successful and more fun to engage in if you knew that you and your teammates all enjoyed a shared sense of inspiration for the idea or outcome?

Practice Your Value

Imagine if your strongest value were practiced every day with those around you. Take generosity as an example. Practicing generosity would equal living one of your highest values authentically. You would demonstrate a generosity of ideas, spirit, sharing, and, of course, giving. Practicing generosity comes naturally to those who hold it as one of their strongest values, and the daily expressions of gratitude could take multiple forms—praising team members efforts, giving financially, or offering time and help to others. Many equate generosity with only money or the donating of money. Generosity of time, wisdom, mentoring, kindness—the applications are numerous—breathes life into people around you. Perhaps you have been the recipient of a generous gift of help or time—nothing monetary, but a teammate or family member going out of their way to help you get to the next step in your work, contributing ideas to solve a problem, or simply listening when you needed to process your thoughts out loud. All these actions demonstrate the practice of generosity.

Take, for example, a teacher who willingly stays after school to help a tentative new reader become more proficient, more confident, and in the end, more competent in the skill of reading. The act of generosity (of time) pays off if the student makes progress, yes. It also pays off as the process of fitting into the classroom with already proficient students becomes easier. That teacher, who brought the joy of reading to life, then becomes an inspiration to both the student and the student's family.

When you have started a fund-raising page or a GoFundMe campaign, isn't that first donation—the person who leads with their generosity—the one that begins building your confidence? It kick-starts the campaign and encourages others to follow. They don't even have to attach a note. Sometimes, the donations are made anonymously. Oftentimes, the note is much more beneficial than the monetary gift, as what better way is there to discover that you have the support for your endeavor from someone who cares?

Try practicing your highest value naturally and abundantly, and watch how that simple expression of a value held dear to you breathes life into those around you. For you, it should come quite naturally, and for those around you, it provides a simple, powerful gift.

Compare this inspiration tool to motivation, which generally constitutes exercising an external stimulant to bring about a shift in action. For example, if the same reading teacher used an external motivator, like a gold star posted on the class reading board or a candy of the student's choice from the teacher's bowl on the desk, would that propel the student to carry on better than the internal drive created by inspiring confidence or competence? Ask yourself this question: When I come up with an idea that I love, do I act on it more powerfully than when someone else suggested (or insisted) upon a course of action for me to take? Generally, we run with our own ideas simply because they are just that—our own rather than someone else's.

Inspire. Breathe life into those around you. Do it authentically, simply by living your highest values and prerogatives. With that level of authenticity, your tool of inspiration will serve you and your team very well indeed.

LEADERSHIP AS A POWERFUL TOOL

If inspiration breathes life into people—individually and collectively—how, then, does leadership differ? That is, how and when do you utilize leadership as a tool instead of inspiration?

Again, let's consider the background and etymology of the word *lead*. The word comes from a German root and means "to guide." Other distinctions include "to march at the head of," "go before as a guide," "accompany and show the way," and "carry on." Do you show the way physically, demonstratively, and ethically? Do you march at the head of the troops? Do you carry on, especially when challenges present themselves? In its earliest usage, the leader held the flag at the front of a battle or procession. Do you carry the flag for your team, organization, or family? Leaders do so—willingly.

In its purest form, leadership always shows up as transformational. That is, we are changed for having followed the leader. We have simply become different—better or worse—than when we started. Leadership takes us to places that we would not go otherwise. We willingly follow a leader. Notice what happens when we are forced or required to follow a leader we did not choose, such as a corrupt politician or CEO or a team leader in the position via nepotism or favoritism. We tolerate but do not fully follow a leader of this sort, as their ability to transform us is compromised by a lack of ethics, direction, validity, or ability.

Authentic leaders rarely concern themselves with getting credit. They gladly share it with their team. Again, this sharing of credit and staying out front in a manner that others want to follow works much more powerfully than imposing an external stimulant upon individuals and teams. So how can *you* lead?

In the end, there is only one manner of authentic leadership: being yourself! Connect with your highest values and talents (I call it your Genius), and simply live those values and talents every day. When you lead by being yourself, you lead authentically. You can be vocal or quiet. You can be action oriented or a deep thinker. The attributes matter little as long as they are authentic to who you are. You will have people follow your lead out of respect and admiration for who their leader is becoming as a full expression of his highest values. Regardless of your highest values, people follow those who live their values every day, even when they do not necessarily share the exact values with their leader. Live your values and exercise your talents, and you lead authentically, in a manner that others will want to follow.

Again, when compared to imposing an incentive or external stimulant to create action, authentically derived leadership presents an incredibly powerful tool for making concrete progress. People follow out of choice rather than from a reaction to stimulus.

THE LEADERSHIP FLY IN THE OINTMENT

Have you ever noticed how many *New York Times* best-selling books exist on leadership and leadership models? Some are autobiographical stories of how a business or political leader accomplished some feat or achievement. Others are *Harvard Business Review*–type case studies detailing the latest research on the most effective way to lead. Often a magic number is part of the process, such as "the seven steps to better leadership" or "the five required attributes to become a more effective leader." Most include a recipe of sorts that will supposedly show the reader how to become a leader according to an author's model.

If you've read one, did you find that it contradicted the last one you read? Funny how that works, that one year the most popular or best-selling leadership model becomes the one that companies want to teach and implement into their organization and teams. The next year, we all attend training or create a study group around the *new* best approach to leadership, or the three steps, versus the five or seven steps, to effective leadership. The game never ends, and the theme of leadership continues to draw lots of attention, as we lack great leaders in our society and our businesses. The new models will not cease to show up on best-seller lists. Read all of them, if you like.

There's a catch with all of these models: None of us are wired like the author who created or espoused the latest and greatest leadership model. If you led like the author, you would need to be just like that author in many other aspects—same personality, same core values, perhaps even the same type of business. Just combining those three factors, the chances of you looking, talking, or acting like the creator of that leadership model are more far-fetched than winning the lottery!

Are you introverted (or extroverted) like the author of the last best-selling leadership book you read? Do you marinate on decisions, as one author might, or shoot from the hip, as another author promotes as his leadership "secret"? Do you tell stories? Use charts, graphs, and statistics? If you are a charts-and-graphs person who "learns to lead better" by telling great stories, chances are you will end up telling lots of pretty average or mediocre stories, because that is not your strong suit. The key here is that you can listen to and learn from all kinds of leadership tactics and success stories, and for you to lead in any capacity, you will most likely have to develop the authentic style that represents most fully who you are at your core.

Why learn to become someone you are not? Learning someone else's model—custom-made for them but not you—sounds incredibly exhausting, like trying to motivate instead of inspire people.

If you are a "thinker" and realize that deciding with your gut equals one of the keys to a specific popular leadership model, my guess is that your stress level will rise significantly and your decision-making ability will deteriorate dramatically if you make this shift. It only makes sense because you are going against the grain of how you are hardwired. If an advantage you hold is your ability to consider decisions fully before making them, and suddenly you are making decisions in rapid-fire fashion, watch out! In short, you are not being your authentically best or most powerful self, and when that occurs, trouble often follows.

There is one simple manner of leadership and inspiration that works with every human being on the planet: embracing your most cherished values, discovering your Genius, and living through those two ingredients.

Values are easier than your Genius. My guess is that you already know your values and may even know them in order of priority. My own, in ranked order, stand as follows: generosity, encouragement, and boldness. Certainly, these are not yours and probably should not be. Your values are just as powerful, and they custom fit to you.

Here's a dirty little secret about your values. Many clients tell me their highest-held values and proceed to list many that are expected. By expected, I mean that the values are expected as a reasonable standard for any human being and, as such, do not mean much. Take, for example, the value called honesty. If you are dishonest, you will have no close friends, you will most likely have no spouse or partner, and you will lose your job in relatively short order. To hold true to the idea of being honest simply reflects a basic societal standard that we impose on any friend, spouse, or employee. In short, you get no extra credit for expected values.

Here's how you know that a value is expected. First, there is no medal for it. We issue medals for courage, valor, achievement, and so forth. We do not issue medals for these expected values: integrity, loyalty, honesty, or fairness. Think about it. Are you expected to be fair? Of course you are, so you get no credit for that. Live from and according to your highest values and you have a great start on inspiring and leading naturally.

Your Genius is a bit more difficult and generally requires

another trained person to uncover well. (Chapter 6 has more on discovering your Genius.) Consider this idea: Contained in your DNA is a singular gift of unique talent that you alone possess on the planet. This talent combines with the customized manner in which you bring it forth (that is, how you bring it forth) and also includes your Why, or your purpose on Earth.

Find your singular gift of talent, and inspire and lead using that as the foundation. You will be living your highest talent and beliefs simultaneously, and your leadership and inspiration will be completely authentic rather than someone else's *New York Times* best-selling approach that does not fit you very well.

Either way, the two powerful tools—inspiration and leadership—are very different though fueled by the same ingredient, authenticity. Each will serve you effortlessly, rather than exhausting you with a constant need to motivate people.

Oscar Wilde said it best: "Be yourself. Everyone else is taken."

CHAPTER 6

The Transformative Qualities of Genius

YOU PROBABLY HAVE one person in your life who possesses admirable and noticeable talent. You only wish you could do what they do and do it with the ease with which they do it. You likely both admire and envy them.

I know that person too. We all do. They seem to glide through life effortlessly. They also seem to enjoy every day, even every moment. What if that person were you? What if you were secretly (or openly) admired and envied for that specific way you are able to pull off that *one thing* with such ease? Chances are you are that person for many people and have never realized it. When you enter a certain realm of activities, you excel like no other. You look like a genius.

Truth is, you *are* a genius. You are a genius because you possess a genius-level talent. We all do. The trick tends to be recognizing, acknowledging, accepting, and then fully utilizing that one high-level talent in a manner that expands what is possible for you every day. Genius™ works that way and, as such, far exceeds any amount of motivation or outside stimulus you might otherwise engage in order to succeed. Exercise and engage it, and it expands. Dismiss it, and it becomes like a doorstop—useful to a point but with limited impact on the world.

WHAT EXACTLY IS GENIUS?

Consider a crime scene that contains DNA samples that have been left in the form of saliva, blood, or sweat. Now consider that the same crime scene has clearly visible fingerprints. Forensic scientists could quickly and easily identify exactly who was present at the scene because they could prove that both the DNA and the fingerprints belong to one individual on the planet. Science is so precise and our DNA and fingerprints are so unique that no other human being in the history of mankind has ever exhibited the same genetic blueprint as anyone else.

Why, then, would it be so odd to imagine that each human being also holds a talent so unique and so highly developed that no other human being in the history of our time on Earth has ever held that same talent? It makes sense, doesn't it? We already have the genetic uniqueness in the form of DNA (our unseen blueprint) and through fingerprints, our outward "signature." Why would our world-class, unique talent, then, not be contained in every cell of our body? The answer quite probably points to the idea that our highest talents are embedded into every cell in our body. I call that Genius, and you have one as unique to you as mine is to me. Your Genius came as "factory equipment," and you "got what you got." I did too.

The trick becomes embracing what you received in a fashion so that you live your life through your Genius rather than against it. Living through your Genius expands your life's possibilities, opportunities, and enjoyment. Wishing for a different Genius contracts and eliminates possibilities, opportunities, and enjoyment and makes life much more of a struggle. One way creates abundance, and the other way creates scarcity.

Whatever talent you got comes as a complete gift, and it came to you free of charge. If you're spiritual, consider it the greatest gift of talent from God. If you embrace a more scientific approach, you won the lottery—big time! Both methodologies work equally well in describing the uniqueness, power, and beauty of Genius.

Perhaps you have no idea what your talent is. Or perhaps you have a sense but not much more. If you're lucky, you work in and around your Genius every day. If this is the case, con-gratulations! If not, let's get you connected to the opportuni-ties afforded by knowing, embracing, and implementing the incredibly expansive qualities associated with doing the one thing on the planet you were gifted to do.

Keep in mind that Genius does not constitute a profession. Genius is neither your IQ nor your SAT score (even if you had a perfect score!). It's not your aptitude in science or math. It's not your ability to do sudoku or complete the *New York Times* Sunday crossword puzzle.

Genius consists of your singular gift of super-high-level tal-ent embedded in every fiber of your being—your DNA, if you will. You received this talent as "factory equipment," and it explains why siblings with the same two parents can be so radically different in both personality and talents. One might be an introverted computer type, while the other is an extro-verted artsy type. In simple terms, they were given completely different talents by, I would suggest, design and for a very specific reason.

Genius appears at the intersection of beauty and power and, in its purest form, creates a field of abundance and unlimited expansion for those who choose to embrace it. Here are a few common phrases that describe playing in your Genius: "in the zone," "flow," "effortless," "feels like play." Genius is also quite attractive—people want to partner with, hire, and engage genius-level talent . . . which means they want to hire, engage, and utilize *your* talent!

Compare that to anything managerial or motivational. Even if you have no energy at work today, your Genius comes so naturally that you could outperform anyone at their highest level of motivation in the same task or role.

ATTRIBUTES THAT SURROUND GENIUS

Ever notice how some people seem to succeed without much stress, effort, or sweat, while others struggle in the same role or task? Chances are one person is working in, around, and through their Genius, and the other is working through a methodology connected to training, process, skills, or motivation. Both may get the job done. One will naturally perform at a higher level and enjoy the process much more.

Why? Noting the attributes and characteristics that surround Genius helps to explain succinctly. Here are some features:

- **Passion or joy**—You love to do this and could do it all day long, every day, and be very happy.

- **Effortlessness**—In (and around) your Genius, results come without much effort, as you hold the talent necessary for great success. It comes naturally.

- **Specificity of talent**—Genius = a singular, high-level talent, not a role or job.

- **Continual improvement with use**—In short, the more you engage and challenge your Genius, the more it improves. You begin to relish big challenges in your field of Genius, and you expand possibilities.

- **An expansive playing field**—Although your talent is super specific, the playground or playing field to utilize and engage your Genius is incredibly abundant and expands with use.

- **Team Genius**—Teams that explore, discover, and engage their cumulative Team Genius outperform those that simply work well together. Consider what it might take to uncover or discover the power of combining multiple Geniuses on one team.

What about areas where we have no Genius at all? Can we develop a genius level of talent? Great question. Thanks for asking.

For me, anything mechanical poses a great challenge. Given a simple "Saturday morning fix-it project," I end up at the hardware store three or four times buying extra tools to correct the secondary mess made by having little aptitude, energy, or intuition as to how to change a washer on a leaky faucet. Invariably, after spending obscene amounts of money to change out a $0.50 washer, I call a plumber to fix the pipe I broke, fix the hole in the sheetrock, and clean up the water damage caused by breaking a pipe and poking a hole in the wall.

Could I learn to do this project correctly? Yes. Will I ever possess genius-level talent in this realm? Never. Could I get really motivated to take on a project like this? Yes, and that makes the prospect even more dangerous. Was last year's office holiday party set up by a highly motivated individual who holds limited talent in designing a fun evening that includes all employees and spouses? Holding no particular talent for any task does not make me any less of a human being, just not the guy to help with the installation of your new deck or kitchen countertops. I'll make sandwiches and lemonade when it comes to contributing to that project.

I was raised by an automotive engineer who routinely built additions and remodels of our family home simply by working on weekends. No formal plans. No additional tools. No trade specialists hired. He loved to do this, was very capable, and seemed happiest when adding utility and value to our family home. Different guy, different talent. He is my dad, and that makes little difference with respect to what talents he possesses and what talents I possess. We got what we got in terms of

Genius. His high-level talents in building also lent themselves well toward his profession as an engineer.

Is it any wonder that he gravitated to the field of designing engines? The two (home construction and auto engineering) are connected well enough, and although I never knew my dad's exact Genius, I did know it showed up in and around mechanical things.

And in case you're curious, no gender holds any particular talent dictated by societal norms. For example, women are not confined to super-high-level talent that would lead to having or raising children, organizing, scheduling, or running a bake sale. Nor are men limited to fixing or building things with their hands, hunting, or leadership. A talent is a talent and devoid of any gender biases.

THE THREE COMPONENTS OF A GENIUS STATEMENT

A Genius Statement outlines your entire Genius and holds three components:

1. **What**—This is the simplest gift of talent, spoken as an action. This is the raw, powerful, and beautiful talent you were given at birth. You cannot change *what* you got. It also = *what* you give to or do for others.

It sounds like this: "My Genius is doing the specific activity of . . . "

2. **How**—This is the unique methodology you have developed, honed, and refined over the course of your lifetime. It = *how* you do *what* you do. In the age-old conversation of nature and nurture, your *how* falls almost entirely into the nurture camp. Your entire lifetime, perhaps by design, has been the playground for developing your unique delivery of your high-level talent. Your How sounds like this: "I do this by Step 1, Step 2, and Step 3."

3. **Why**—You received a great gift of talent and have spent a lifetime developing it. Ever consider that you might have been given this talent (as opposed to another) for a specific reason? In its simplest form, your Why = your purpose on the planet—the reason you exist. Other than that, it does not have much use. Your Why sounds like this: "I do this because I believe . . ."

Here is what a complete Genius Statement sounds like. This is my own.

"My Genius is creating seemingly impossible outcomes that address multiple diverse agendas (my What). I do this by designing one unifying game (Step 1), enrolling all the participants

(Step 2), and then constantly adjusting the game to ensure that each player gets exactly what they came for (Step 3) (my How). I do this because I believe that when we play boldly together, everyone wins BIG (my Why)!"

Could I have found or created this statement online or by taking one of the many really good, eerily accurate personality or assessment tests? I suggest not. Genius is way too highly specific. It contains *your* language. The articulation of the specific talent does not come from a drop-down list of possibilities that you choose. It comes from an expressive process of you outlining episodes of peak performance—where your What, How, and Why were all fully aligned.

You have had episodes where these three elements have all been in place at one time. The trick is, you may or may not have recognized that you were in the presence of your Genius. Our tendency as human beings is to dismiss these episodes as the result of good fortune, dumb luck, other people's contributions, or a myriad of other explanations for great results occurring.

Truth is, when it comes to your Genius, you have no equal on the planet, and you will produce fabulous results every time, even if the challenge increases every time. There is no ceiling on the level of your talent. You simply have to know what it is and then place yourself in the arenas where your specific Genius is needed and wanted most.

There's a wise saying about capital, and it applies to Genius as well: "Capital will always go where it's welcome and stay where it's well treated." Capital is not just money. It's also talent and ideas. They, too, will go where they're welcome and stay where they are well treated. Genius works the same way. Go to where your Genius will be welcomed most and stay in the arenas where it is treated best!

Particularly as it relates to the Why part of your Genius statement, expanding your life's contribution, joy, play, and happiness will be directly proportional to the amount of time you invest in activities closely connected to your life's purpose, your Why. Even if you are not *using* your highest talent, when you are working in conjunction with your life's purpose, almost any form of activity has high meaning.

Go to where your purpose, or Why, is treated best!

WHAT THE HECK IS YOUR GENIUS?

How the heck do you find your Genius, how do you know it's right, and how do you design your life to take advantage of it?

In working with more than 7,500 clients in the pursuit of discovering their highest-level, unique talent, I have learned that your Genius cannot be concocted or discovered with a formula, with an online test, or by picking and choosing components that feel or sound right. We all possess blind spots as human beings, and we all project our desires or wishes when learning about ourselves. If we are allowed to simply choose what we think might be our Genius, there is a chance we could get it right . . . but more often than not, we simply choose what looks most needed, wanted, or wished for rather than what is actually present.

The methodology for uncovering or discovering your Genius is simple, takes about two hours, and is very accurate. Why? Because it involves a series of stories you are led to "uncover" from your history that fit a specific pattern where your What (your high-level talent), your How (your unique way of producing results with that talent), and your Why (your most fundamental core belief) all align. How many of these stories do you have? Probably dozens. We need four or five to see the clear patterns that show up around you when your What, How, and Why are all aligned. That alignment of super-high-level talent and your Highest Purpose can beat any form of training, development, or motivation that your team leader throws at you.

What has shown up in cases where these three key elements exist simultaneously is a clearly surprising result that occurs at the time. The result will look surprising to you but predictable to others around you once you can recognize, own, and then duplicate the criteria needed for that talent to expand and flourish.

Sounds simple, and in many ways it is. The hardest part is

not figuring it out. Sadly, a surprisingly difficult part is that even after discovering their individual Genius, many people simply cannot own the power and beauty contained in their talent, so they never put it to full use. Occasionally they will have peak episodes, and those will be due to random interactions with their Genius rather than a full strategic employment of their greatest gift of talent.

What might this look like? In my case, I thrive in arenas where there is little or no chance of success—long shots, if you will. That atmosphere simply arouses my talent and gives notice that it is time to play—expansion, if you will, of a sleeping or latent talent.

Once there is a "seemingly impossible outcome" or long shot, then everything else kicks in, and I am off to the races. More often than not, we (all involved) create a big success where there was no prior possibility. In short, everyone wins, which is why I play in the first place—my Why.

As mentioned, though, your Genius will not come from a formula, a test, reading, researching, or interviewing others. It can only come from your own experiences and will contain your own words.

THE DIRTY LITTLE SECRET ABOUT GENIUS
AND EXPANSION

Genius is not for everyone. Just ask an "average" person. Discovering your Genius is really fun. Owning the full power of it takes some courage—the courage to lead a great life in which you utilize your greatest gift of talent. Your life then will expand in relation to the contribution you can make, the impact you can have, and the joy you will give and receive as a part of living the expansive life of Genius.

Dyana is a good friend who discovered her Genius. Dyana's Genius is to champion the unique gifts of others so that they may claim their own divinity, because she fundamentally believes that we are all connected. Can you guess what she did for a career? Minister? Nope, she's an atheist. Therapist? Nope. She runs (or ran) her own executive search firm. She was a headhunter. She worked only for commission, hustled a lot, was super-capitalistic, and had a Genius that was wholly spiritual!

If you think about it, Dyana's Genius would be a great way to do effective headhunting (okay, "executive search-ing") because she would have the natural talent to make sure that the candidates were great fits for the culture they were being hired into, and vice versa for the firms she placed people into. She was good at what she did . . . and also realized that once she started to own her Genius, her contribution and calling were not as well served by her career choice as perhaps another, more meaningful choice. In short, her last executive search would be for herself.

Problem was, Dyana knew that executive searching was not her calling—just a pretty good fit for her high-level talent of connecting people with their own divinity. Here's where the transformation fit, and it may for you too. Like you, Dyana took the courageous step to live the full life connected to her Genius rather than using her Genius as best she could in what she was doing. She made the decision to invest the rest of her life into a career—a calling—that would take much better advantage of her high-level talent, yes, but would also connect perfectly with her Why. Dyana sold her executive search firm and had enough funds to transition into coaching. She did much training and certification, and her talents fit naturally into the new field she chose.

The trick is that Dyana had the courage to pursue a new career in an expansive field, in which she could contribute (and receive) much more than she could before.

Does this mean you need to change careers to own your Genius? Not at all. The courage to redesign how you take on your career, your specific role on your team, your volunteer opportunities, or the way you relate to friends and family is the same courage Dyana employed to redesign her career. It's a simple, powerful, courageous choice to live the most expansive life you can live. The rewards pay off for the rest of your life! Beats being motivated to do a job, role, or career you fundamentally are not well suited for.

—

CHAPTER 7

Using Directives to Shift and Drive Effective Behavior

CLEARLY, KNOWING YOUR individual's, team's, and organization's Highest Purpose or Why rests as a foundational move that fosters a more dynamic and healthy culture. Having coached teams and organizations for over a decade, I have seen that simply having these directives in place does not ensure that "people problems" go away. Culture, after all, consists first and foremost of people, and given our tendency to be erratic at times, people problems never seem to disappear totally.

To illustrate, when I used to visit a Fortune 50 software company near Seattle, the team we were hired to work with would start off every session in much the same way, whether we were on campus for consecutive days or whether we saw them only once per quarter. My partners and I were hired to get the team back into high performance. Essentially, they were not fulfilling very well on their overall team objective or the most important projects. Coaching was prescribed, contracted, and paid for. We would then show up, and the initial dialogue went something like this at 8:30 a.m.:

Team member: "What the f—k do you guys know about software?"

Me: "Well, nothing actually, so I guess we can agree that we have not been hired to solve any software issues. Why else might we be here?"

At that point, the aggressive team member would quietly take a seat, realizing that the people issues the team members were having stemmed not one iota from their extensive knowledge of software but rather from their poor treatment of people. By midmorning, that same team would start making progress, and by the end of the first day, the team expressed thanks to us for helping them address challenges that they either could not see or could see clearly enough but just did not want to address publicly.

Who knew coaches could help so much? Well, as a direct

result of many years of work focused on watching individuals clearly not living up to a company's stated values, my partners and I realized that telling people how to be—for instance, honest or creative—rests clearly in their interpretation or viewpoint of what is acceptable for them. In contrast, telling people exactly what to do leaves much less doubt as to whether they are living up to the highest values, ethics, and desired culture of the organization. Turns out we *do* much better than we *be*.

While we were coaching software teams in Seattle, the CEO of that Fortune 50 company appeared on one of the financial channels. When asked what the core values were for his firm, he misstated two of the five values that employees were being asked to live by!

We resigned from coaching that firm within three months, having solved the mystery of why the company wasn't making any progress. The CEO did not even know the core values, let alone live them. How the heck were any of the more than 100,000 employees expected to figure out the core values, interpret them, and then live them at their highest expression?

That's why directives, or short commands, function so much better than do one-word values stated as aspirations, or ways of being. Directives also trounce motivation in terms of driving accepted behavior, since the directives are clear, are hard to misinterpret, and hold as a foundation the same aspirational value that serves as the basis for the directive. Let's look at an example so you do not waste time motivating people to do the right thing.

Let's take the core values from another super-successful company—one that is a household name. Their language is copied directly from their website. Here's how it reads:

- **Leadership:** The courage to shape a better future

- **Collaboration:** Leverage collective genius

- **Integrity:** Be real

- **Accountability:** If it is to be, it's up to me

- **Passion:** Committed in heart and mind

- **Diversity:** As inclusive as our brands

- **Quality:** What we do, we do well

Pick "leadership," since it sits on the top of their list. If the CEO or the HR trainer invites, suggests, or insists that you need to have "the courage to shape a better future," what will that mean for you in your role? Is the courage to shape a better future for my own future? For my family's future? The customers? The manager who gives me a performance review?

The language is flowery and rather poetic, and the question

remains: Does leadership as a core value resonate with each person on the team in the manner stated? Furthermore, if the intended meaning is not terribly clear to the employees, does the organization have to train and invest time together to ferret out the actual intended meaning? If the needs-clarifying process is part of their hiring and training procedure and if the intended outcome is not clear, how could it become a catalytic factor driving great results and profits in this highly successful company?

Consider the language surrounding passion ("committed in heart and mind") and integrity ("be real," whatever that means). As an employee of this company, if I were asked to be real, would my manager, coworkers, or the leadership team like what I expressed as real to me in my life? That could include NASCAR, extreme religious views, sexual orientations that might make others uncomfortable, or positions on politics that divide instead of unite people. All these positions ostensibly would be both protected and encouraged as part of being real.

The company in question is none other than *Coca-Cola*, one of the top five most recognized brands in the world. If Coke doesn't quite have this down pat, then you can see the challenge for you and me. Let's clarify your needs and make your team stronger right now!

Imagine if Coke took as a high (or its highest) value the new theme of vitality or health. Do you think they could agree on a directive that might lead to the creation of a beverage that could outsell Coca-Cola and promote optimum health? I suspect so. Coke sells billions of dollars' worth of a product that customers enjoy, and Coke does this with rather unclear directives. They rank as an admired company by business leaders, mostly due to their financial soundness, the quality of the management teams, and their profit margins. Employees do not rave about working at Coke. Health officials have banned soft drinks, namely Coke, from many primary and secondary schools based on the detrimental health effects that come with drinking it, namely, obesity. Class action lawsuits against soft drink makers and sin taxes such as those imposed against alcohol and cigarette products have already begun in several states. What might happen to Coke if they directed their resources to an approach that sold incredibly profitable products that helped people rather than created public health issues?

OUR QUEST: AUTONOMOUS TEAM MEMBERS

Remember, our quest here is not to have to resort to a forceful approach to achieving results from team members. No motivation. No contests. No gimmicks. What if our team members align with our team's values and live them by choice, and you and I as team leaders do not have to lord over them? What might your team look like if it were more autonomous and driven by purpose and values rather than by you motivating, enticing, or perhaps berating them each day? Well, let's do that together right now.

Take your team or organization's top three or top five stated values. They probably exist, as Coca-Cola's and so many other companies' do, as one-word values or perhaps as the value combined with a short description. For fun, we'll use some of Coke's values and bring them to life in a way that drives autonomy of team members; that is to say, there would be no confusion over *what* I was supposed to do or *how* I was supposed to do it. This clarity would exist, regardless of whether I had a good night's sleep, felt like doing my job today, or thought my boss was kind of a jerk. We're doing here, not interpreting, much as the military does not give much energy or concern to whether you like the order you were just given by your drill sergeant. You are simply expected to understand and fulfill the order.

To start with, I will discard two of the values that Coke sets forth, as they are considered expected. By expected, I mean that you or I are fully expected to live with integrity and accountability. While you're at it, you can add honesty, loyalty, openness, and fairness. The simple litmus test to know whether a value is expected? *If I were not this way, would I get fired, divorced, or have any friends at all?*

Consider "openness" a core value. Not one job candidate has ever aced a job interview by stating how open or open-minded they were, and in fact, no employer gives high marks to open-minded people. Employers, potential spouses, friends, and colleagues expect and require a sense of open-mindedness, so you get zero credit for living out this value. An even easier standard might be this: If there is no such award for the stated value, then it might be expected. There are awards for valor, courage, achievement, creativity, impact—the list goes on. There are no awards for honesty. None exist for integrity or loyalty. Your employer pays you, for goodness' sake. Of course you are expected to be loyal! Setting up your company based on an expected value means that you get routine results.

So, back to Coke. Let's start with "passion" as a reasonable core value. Coke even gives further clarification, namely, "committed in heart and mind." You and I are invited or asked by Coke's leadership team to be committed in heart and mind. So here is the key question: When it comes time for our performance review, how do you or I assess that I have been (fully) committed in heart and mind? Furthermore, what the heck am I expected to be committed to?

The rule is simple: If a National Geographic film crew could not repeatedly witness our actions on tape if they followed us around for a month, then the core value has little relevant or useful meaning. You and I would simply argue about how committed I felt or about all the little things that demonstrated how committed I really was or about how much I felt committed in my heart. In the end, there is simply no way to prove that I was being committed in heart and mind. It's impossible to prove by watching the Nat Geo film.

Let's turn this around. Rather than asking you and me to "be" a certain way, what if we were directed or commanded—much as an army sergeant would do—that we "do" a certain thing repeatedly? Would a film crew be able to catch our actions demonstrably on film? Would they be able to prove that we were doing the specific commanded or demanded action? I suspect that anyone might be able to vouch for our actions. If that were the case, then why not *command* the one recurrent action that represented what it meant to be committed in heart and mind? Notice that if we are commanding or demanding, the linguistic structure will almost certainly have to start with an action verb. Directives always start with an action verb. How about some of these proposals for what Coke might command if they wanted to ensure that we acted in a manner that demonstrated "passion"?

- Give your best effort every day.

- Exercise your talents at their highest level.

- Contribute to your own results and those of others at all times.

- Love what you do. Love the people you do it with.

The possibilities are endless. The key here (and let's check it) would be this: The film crew can witness this activity or mandate simply by watching the tape of us at work. To the extent that we did what was expected, does our manager or teammate care whether or not we were motivated to do so? Probably not. Do either of them care whether we felt a high state of motivation to do what was commanded or demanded? Again, probably not. The results follow because we are doing it, not feeling it.

If we simply lived the directive and did what was demanded and expected, most people problems would simply disappear in large measure. Our being would reflect in our doing, and our doing would ensure that we were living our highest core values. The underlying core value for Coke would not change—namely, "passion." But rather than speaking about passion, we would simply focus on what everyone agreed upon in terms of a direction or action. The directive, in turn, would ensure a very high compliance rate for the desired aspirational core value. Passion would begin to show up more predictably because we exercised actions that create it on a daily basis. No more need to motivate, entice, or manipulate. Simply do.

Let's try the exercise again with "collaboration," which Coke describes with "leverage collective genius." Again, the wording sounds great until we ask some simple questions:

- What is our collective genius? Do we know our respective individual geniuses?

- How are we allowed (or supposed) to leverage our own and collective talents and geniuses?

- Who is in charge of this process? By that I mean, who is responsible to make sure it occurs?

Imagine the new employee orientation session, Day 1, where all this leveraging of collective genius gets described, taught, and with luck, agreed to by the newbies. When they enter the actual working environment, say Day 2, selling carbonated sugar water with some citric acid and food coloring added, how exactly do they expect to leverage the collective genius in those around them? Clearly, someone at Coke way back when was a real genius in this model, as the product harms health, promotes diabetes, is super inexpensive to produce, sells like crazy worldwide, and has stable profit margins. I wish I had figured out that recipe for success!

But back to our exercise here—to create a directive or command that we all can do, and by doing it we can (better) ensure that our desired collaboration occurs. Here are a couple of attempts at what it might sound like to command or demand collaboration at Coke or at your team:

- Work with your teammates to produce exponential results.

- Engage the help of others quickly if you face challenges beyond your reach.

- Partner with team members to complete results quicker and easier.

Again, when a film crew can verify that you and I are actually doing what is asked, it matters much less whether we are motivated to complete the task in a specific manner. If we show a tendency to "partner with team members" or to "work with teammates," the film will certainly show that. Would you create results quicker working this way? When might this process actually slow you down? What activities are most conducive to this type of collaborative activity, and which are better done alone? The process can be tested, refined, and updated, all while remaining true to the initial intention of "being collaborative." We can make progress toward improving our directive so that we promote more collaboration among all teammates in the organization.

Directives work primarily because of the linguistic structure. You are not asked to do something. You are told or commanded to do something. That something represents the movement toward a positive result, so simply by doing what you are recurrently asked, you help to promote a positive culture.

Compare this to other manners of living core values, and you eliminate or lessen the need to motivate and even manage team members. The team members become much more effective at discerning the right move to make at many different junctures. In the end, this tool of directives allows you to employ a powerful rather than a forceful tool.

A QUICK TUTORIAL ON CREATING EFFECTIVE DIRECTIVES

You probably know your highest values and might even have them in ranked order. If that's the case, you've got the primer for creating effective directives. The steps are below, but to begin, here are some simple rules for directives. First, they start with an action verb. Rarely does a drill sergeant ask a buck private to do anything. The drill sergeant commands the private to do things. Your directive should do the same. Second, if you cannot logically end your command with an exclamation point, chances are you do not have a strong enough directive.

1. Take your one-word values and put them in priority order. As an example, let's use honesty, creativity, and compassion.

2. Now, let's turn a one-word value into a simple command that would indicate that you are doing what you claim to be doing. For example, if you claim to be honest, what would you command yourself to do? For starters, let's try this: Tell the truth!

3. Once you have your first cut, move to strengthen it. Consider a "good, better, best" process of improvement. "Tell the truth!" is good, but you could always tell the truth and still leave out pertinent details, so as good a start as you have, you could make it better. Let's try: "Tell the truth at all times!" Ah, better, as it commands you to tell the truth everywhere, all the time, to all people, not just when it suits you. Still, I suggest that you could strengthen this even more with a "best" version: "Tell the truth at all times, regardless of the outcome!" Tell the truth even when it may embarrass you or someone else, even when there could be serious repercussions. If you lived at this level of honesty, imagine how your reputation might change. No longer do you simply live by a code of honesty, you have strengthened the original value of honesty to something much more powerful, namely, transparency. You command yourself to tell the truth all the time and then deal with the outcomes afterward, but your willingness

to "come clean" makes effective actions much more possible, even if there is a cleanup, apology, or serious implication involved. This version of your directive commands you to live at the highest level of honesty— the type not seen much in politics, in the media, or even in many companies.

Try this "good, better, best" exercise with each of your prioritized one-word values, and change your values into directives. You will improve and increase your personal power when you do.

CHAPTER 8

Habits Beat Motivation Hands Down

MOTIVATION WORKS GREAT as a catalyst for a more sustainable vehicle. Motivation is supposed to stay in place only until the point where another primary vehicle takes over. It was never intended, at least not based on neuroscience, to sustain us for long periods of time. Motivation functions really well for a second-half rally of a sports team or for a final push in the last few days of the sales quarter. Otherwise, motivation is meant to be replaced as quickly as possible by any number of more suitable tools. We've discussed inspiration and leadership, but several other primary vehicles can take over from motivation in an energetic handoff of power.

Let's say that your team members are now (more) inspired

to take action of their own volition, and you have authentic leadership capabilities in place. Wow! You're off to a great start. Inspired team members and a competent leader will significantly improve your team's chances for success in any project or goal and will also make the daily mood and culture pretty darn enjoyable for most.

It's time we take more specialized tools and add them to the mix. Do we care that your initial motivation is now long forgotten? Not really, as its role is complete; it sparked ideas and initial actions forward. You've started and are looking to improve your success in a key project. A highly recommended set of tools for motivation to hand off to as quickly as possible is (new) habits. Here's why.

If a National Geographic film crew followed you around for a month and captured the activities that you do every single day, you and I would be able to agree that more than 40 percent of everything you do is habitual—which is to say, much less than is fully conscious on your part. You don't think about what you are doing; you simply do it. Effective? Yes, especially when the unconscious actions fall in alignment with your highest values, beliefs, health, happiness, wellness, and overall success in life. To the extent that your habits detract from the life you would like to live, well . . . the momentum shifts in a less than positive direction.

Take the way you lock up your apartment or home when you

leave each day. Do you always hold the keys in your dominant hand? Do you always attempt to turn the knob after you lock up, just to make sure that you safely locked your home? Where do you put the keys once you have locked up? I would be willing to bet that they go into the exact same place every single time. A film crew could verify this by watching you on consecutive days.

If you were ever required to lock your door with your nondominant hand, the film crew from National Geographic would need to invest a far greater amount of time filming you. Most likely, your actions would become very conscious, like eating, writing, or brushing your teeth with your nondominant hand. Your competence toward achieving your desired results would not improve much with a healthy dose of motivation. Habitual actions actually facilitate effectiveness and efficiency and as such are not affected much positively or negatively by motivation. We simply perform those actions in a less than fully conscious state of mind. They get done without much thought, acceptance, or introspection.

In the end, your habits, both good and bad, function far better than does your motivation, since unconscious behavior runs you like a computer software program—without human intervention or emotion—rather than with conscious thought or a thorough reflection on whether the activity fits your highest values. To the extent that your habits shift, so too do your outcomes—whether in improving health, saving money, locking your door, or brushing your teeth. To the extent that you shift your habits, you shift your expected outcomes—for better or for worse.

HANDING OFF TO (NEW) HABITS

When you use your highest intentions, values, and goals to serve as the spark for (re)designing your habitual actions, progress occurs much quicker and, more importantly, more powerfully. Your actions begin to more fully collaborate with your highest values, purpose, and sense of contribution—for your life and for the lives of others. You have intentionally rethought, proposed, and agreed upon a new, more effective way that you would like to act all (or most) of the time. Good for you! This is the first healthy step of your motivation handing off to successful, healthier, more effective habits—that fall in line with your ideals, values, goals, and purpose.

Let's say you are super motivated to finally take off those 30 extra pounds, which will get you to your desired target weight. You gathered all the motivation you could muster to get to the gym or boot camp for two full days—until all your motivation got thunked on the head by the challenge and post-workout soreness of those darn squats and sit-ups. Truth is, motivation was never intended to last much longer than your first day or two at a gym. The power of life forces conspiring against you far outweighs the conspiracy called life events, which are designed to support your temporary highly motivated state. Rain and cold at 5:45 a.m., not to mention darkness and an hour less sleep, all conspire to create enough resistance and, over a very short period of time, will completely shred most forms of motivation.

You got off the hook already once you learned that diet presents the more important and effective method to lose weight, so working out is not the primary catalyst to take off the pounds. Woo-hoo! You just need to shift (as little of) what you eat and drink as would be required to have the weight magically fall off. Truth is, if a doctor gave you 90 days to lose 30 pounds to keep from keeling over, you would likely find all the necessary information to achieve that outcome in just a few minutes online. The information is readily accessible and not just in one eating strategy or diet plan. Caloric laws work the same for everyone, and they are not too difficult to understand. Eat the right foods. Avoid the wrong foods. Move more.

Motivation, in the form of the fear of dying, would work well in that life-or-death scenario, perhaps even for the full 90 days of your new workout routine. The time limit is not the primary catalyst; the dying part is. You either achieve your desired weight goal or you do not, with a very clear "pass-fail" dynamic in place. Your (fear-based) motivation might last for a full 90 days in this dire circumstance—much longer than most less threatening situations.

For those of us losing weight for vanity, for improved energy, for more vibrant long-term health, or for any other valid reason, motivation generally falls apart pretty quickly, primarily because the consequences of not losing the weight simply do not present such a serious consequence as the prospect of dying would. If we lost only fifteen pounds or lost the weight more slowly than we initially thought or yo-yoed our way back and forth between losing the weight and gaining it back, our motivation would ebb and flow with the fit of our skinny jeans. We would adjust and note the frustration with our slower-than-desired progress.

Now consider the idea that our initial motivation to lose 30 pounds quickly hands off to a series or set of newly designed, healthier (eating) habits. The habits would most likely not have been in place already; otherwise you would not have the weight loss challenge! Quite to the contrary, detrimental or clearly unhealthy habits (at least for weight loss) would most likely rule the outcome that has become your waistline. You are ready to relook at, redesign, and replace poor health and exercise habits such that you literally become a different person.

Imagine that you designed a set of habits that by themselves would all but ensure progress toward the desired weight loss. What might they look like? How about these options to start:

- Eat a protein salad at lunch with balsamic vinegar and olive oil.

- Replace soda, juices, and all alcoholic drinks with high-alkaline filtered water.

- Eat only organic meats, eggs, and vegetables.

- Replace after-dinner sweets and snacks with raw nuts.

You could come up with a long list of your own suggestions. Weight-loss experts know the laws of caloric science, and in the end, low to no carbohydrates and sugar replaced by (clean) protein, organic vegetables, raw nuts, and (some) fruits promotes a system in our bodies in which stored fat calories begin to be burned for use by your body as energy. The pounds fall off quite quickly and naturally, and your skinny jeans begin to fit again.

In the end, improved habits, designed to achieve exactly what your outcome should look like, work far more effectively than does any sort of high state of motivation, even if that comes attached to motivational quotes, podcasts, or daily affirmations. Remember, your brain works much like a microprocessor, and "programming" that operating system with strategic, thoughtfully designed activities that you would like to employ on autopilot presents a far more reliable system for change than would emotionally charged activities that can shift day to day, based on the outdoor temperature at 5:30 that morning.

Motivation is designed, in the end, to work for the short run rather than manage our long-term thinking, actions, or intended results. The handoff, quickly, from motivation to a more effective medium provides the necessarily powerful move. Habits present a simple powerful move to make—whether for an individual to lose weight or for a team to create faster, more productive coordination between and among team members.

When you create, design, redesign, or transform habits as a team, the process works very much the same. In the end, many of the newly agreed-upon habits begin to form the basis of systems or processes—completion of the same outcome, to the same standards, by all players on the team. If you could create or shift just *one* habit that impacted the entire team, what would that one habit be?

In the end, the most powerful shifts in habits that affect teams come from what matters most to each of us as individuals and all of us in unison. Does our culture dictate one set of actions versus another simply because of what we believe? If your culture is well designed and articulated, it should.

Does how we agree to treat each other or how we agree to treat our customers and clients present a simple, powerful opportunity to "upgrade" a habit for every member of our team? Here's a simple example from a Fortune 500 company that brought in a new COO to help with customer delight. The company in question, a copier and business machine firm, stood as the primary player in their industry. Over time, they had simply gotten a bit too big and seemed to lose connection to what each of their customers really desired. In the end, the price to pay to purchase this firm's product ended up much higher than cheaper upstart (read: foreign) competitors, who were both more innovative and much more aggressive on price. Profits lagged. Layoffs ensued.

The COO installed a newly transformative habit and began to check it with his team leaders: *Every day, every person who works here will have direct contact with at least one customer.*

The idea was simple. This COO realized in short order that his entire organization had developed the organizational habit of "hiding out" and had lost contact and connection with what really mattered to each one of their customers. He knew that they could not remedy that in a boardroom or with better training but needed to address it on a people-to-people basis. His team members needed to connect with the customers personally.

The pushback started almost immediately and came first from the controller, who reasoned that his role simply did not require direct contact with customers. The COO asked, "Why could you not be of great service to one of our customers? You may not know that much about the technical aspects of our product, but couldn't you be of service to customers on how to run their business more profitably?"

The initiative worked. The COO knew that a "rally" or a prize or an incentive would not turn around the culture or performance of the giant firm. He recognized, primarily because he had not ascended from within the organization, that his organization needed to transform their habits to match their values and culture. A simple, radical, transformational habit—just one—worked to reconnect every one of his team members to their biggest asset: their customers. The initiative, founded on one new habit, turned around the company and returned them to profitability and, more importantly, to a predictable future.

Again, what one habit might you propose for every person in your organization or team that would begin to shift or transform your results? Would it affect relationships, performance, consistency, morale, or revenue? Once you decide upon the first habit to employ, what might you follow that with?

Partner motivation with healthy habits and your highest values and succeed. Utilize motivation for its intended purpose, with its intended time frame—namely, for a very short period of time—and motivation yields terrific results. Who'd have thunk it that we work better when we do not consciously think? Habits make that possible.

Here's to your newly designed habits.

CHAPTER 9

Single-Minded Focus and Maniacal Tracking

MY WIFE AND I recently watched the documentary *What the Health*, which outlined not only the inconsistencies but also the convoluted relationships between the US Department of Agriculture, the American Cancer Society, the American Diabetes Association, and the Federal Drug Administration. The simple conclusion from the director, outlined quite well in interviews with the heads of these organizations, became pretty darn clear: Most disease exists primarily as a result of contaminated or manipulated food sources. Shift the source of the food and the quality of the food, namely to a vegetarian or vegan diet, and our population would greatly improve our statistically unprecedented rate of debilitating diseases. We would also wean our population off the drugs prescribed to treat diseases such as diabetes, high blood pressure, high cholesterol, and many forms of cancer.

The documentary was both compelling and very convincing in its arguments. In the end, my wife and I were confronted with a simple choice: keep eating as we have been, with a diet heavily centered around meats, and wait for the inevitable consequences to occur, or shift to a more informed and scientifically supported lifestyle. For three days, we simply could not get the documentary out of our heads, including my wife having "vegan nightmares." Our focus on our diets became front and center.

You may have experienced an event, a riveting story, or a newfound paradigm that dramatically shifted your perspective, your choices, and in the end, your primary focus in your business or your life. My wife and I both realized halfway through the film that we would adopt a vegan lifestyle—not something we had considered previously. We could not avoid a "single-minded focus" on the key points of the film, even after conversations with friends who discounted the advantages of a vegan diet. My wife is also a physician, which made our focus and our choice to switch to a health-focused diet that much more inevitable.

Our "foodie" focus, which centered primarily on choosing

high-quality, expensive meat proteins, shifted to a simpler, much clearer focus on overall robust health. We now choose our foods completely by design, we track our food sources, and we favor organic over nonorganic and GMO over non-GMO. All this new "maniacal tracking" of our diet was created in direct pursuit of greatly improved health, of more energy, of healthier blood and cholesterol levels, and of elevated strength, since we are both active, competitive athletes.

So far, the results have lined up as promised, especially the blood work (did I mention that my wife is a physician?) and the reduction in aches and pains associated with inflammation of joints. We track all our performances at workouts, and to our surprise, our strength and endurance numbers have increased in the first two months. These data seemed in opposition to everything we had believed about getting high-quality (meat and egg) protein sources for improved strength and endurance.

When was the last time you altered your choices based upon a newfound realization that shifted your highest outcomes, health, enjoyment, and focus in your life? The changes in practice make a big difference, whether in your health, your career, your spirituality, or your parenting. Creating a single-minded focus and then maniacally tracking your activities and results make all the difference in the outcomes you create.

WHAT THE HECK IS SINGLE-MINDED FOCUS?

Clients in a successful financial planning firm in New York City realized in our individual and team coaching sessions that they were working really hard and raising their revenues at a faster pace than their competitors. The industry revenue growth stood at 9.6 percent, and they were just over 15 percent, so they were doing quite well. The challenge they faced, however, became pretty clear: As individuals and as a team, they were working at a pace that would not allow them to reasonably work any additional hours to raise revenues in the coming year. Their stated goal was to double their revenue in two years, which essentially meant having back-to-back "best years ever," increasing from their current 15 percent revenue growth to over 41 percent revenue growth for the next two years. Something fundamental had to change. They could not drive, motivate, or entice their team members to create such exponentially increased sales results.

I proposed that we employ a simple, powerful tool: single-minded focus. Simply put, single-minded focus involves the deployment of one *catalytic* activity that will drive multiple positive outcomes. At the time we met, the firm in question's leaders had five key initiatives that they managed and kept track of. In essence, they were dividing their focus among five objectives in the pursuit of one key outcome: higher revenues. I flipped the proposition and asserted that focusing on one transformational or catalytic activity would create five or more positive outcomes. They liked the notion, but they were skeptical about the concept. In the end, they decided to try the concept of one single-minded focus.

If they had run out of available hours to work while they were increasing revenues at an above-industry average of 15 percent, they simply could not adopt a strategy of working harder or longer. Their revenue goal would require a strategy where the firm would have to evolve, redesign, or transform. Essentially, they desired a scenario where they would increase revenue by over 41 percent *while working fewer hours*! I insisted on fewer hours, as that criterion forced the required process of innovation and transformation rather than employing a strategy that would prove less sustainable. They agreed that the idea of raising revenues by working people harder would appeal to no one in their firm.

I suggested that the clients needed to design a single-minded focus that if adopted and followed well, would provide the catalyst to ensure that their newly dictated growth level would occur as a predictable result. The clients have been in business for over sixteen years, so why would this concept not have become more obvious earlier? Herein lies the rub, or the blind spot, as it is called in coaching.

The answer exists as a less than obvious answer, especially for clients who work hard, which is true with this great team.

Members of this firm, not surprisingly, embraced hard work as one of their keys to success over the years. Your team probably works really hard as well. Working harder, or at least working longer hours each week, simply would not scale to produce what they wanted and most likely would produce resentment among the team members—a form of diminishing returns on hours worked, if you will.

Eventually, I asked the clients about their sales process, how they obtained referrals, and what percentage of the referrals became long-term paying clients. As it turned out, to start their business, this successful firm took any and all paying clients. Revenue of any kind was welcomed and cherished—even when the newly paying clients did not fit into the firm's ideal client model. This idea that any client is better than no client has deep roots in our Puritanical work ethic as a culture. In a commissioned sales business, this strategy comes about naturally, as young, inexperienced, hungry sales reps take any client versus having no clients at all. At least with a less than ideal client, the young salesperson has a file to work on, a bit of revenue, and someone to follow up with. Hooray! A sale! Culturally, we have learned to accept most paying clients instead of applying any reasonable standards or filters designed to weed out poor-fitting clients.

Those filters might sound something like this: Are we the best firm for this client? Does this client benefit from our product suite and delivery process? Would we love to engage ten more clients just like this one, or would ten more clients just like this one actually create problems for us?

As you might imagine, the answers to these filtering questions simply did not exist. At the beginning of their firm's growth, there was only one filtering question or standard: Are they paying us? Sixteen years later, some sense of discernment existed, where the more sophisticated and profitable clients made the most sense to engage—both for the best interests of the paying clients and also for the best model for the firm. Still, the cultural bias existed, and committed salespeople continued to take on less than ideal clients since they still got compensated, albeit in smaller-than-ideal amounts.

After much discussion, my clients realized that they engaged a little over half of the clients for whom they held a successful initial or "open" meeting—the first meeting to begin their sales and service process. Since most new client prospects had to switch from an existing financial advisory firm to engage our clients, a 50 percent closing rate seemed about right. I then asked about their process for getting the introductions and referrals that led to these new prospects.

To my great surprise, the process for gaining new client introductions was almost entirely organic. By *organic* I mean that the financial advisors held a formal "annual review" with clients where they addressed the clients' overall financial performance of their assets, possible life changes, risks upcoming in the financial markets, and so on. The theory existed that if the financial advisors were taking great care of the investing clients, then the clients would naturally refer friends, family, and associates. To the extent that the firm grew at a faster pace than their competitors, the theory worked well enough. However, in order to grow at a rate just above 41 percent (note: 41.5 percent annual growth for consecutive years is needed to double in that time span), their theory collapsed entirely, especially with my insistence that the 41 percent growth include the provision that they work fewer hours, not more.

I suggested that they peel apart, with a single-minded focus, all the year-to-date data and tracking of the initial open meetings. My simple sense was that the more opens, the higher the growth rate, since 50 percent eventually became paying clients. Focus all the efforts and attention on increasing both the quantity and quality of the opens, and the sales growth would follow automatically. Single-minded focus works like that. It ensures results logically and predictably by changing only one catalytic or transformational activity.

With very simple reviews of each financial advisor's calendared meetings for the year, it was determined that the average number of open meetings per advisor, on average, was on pace for 26—essentially 2 per month, 1 of which would result in a new client. In my coaching practice, I have long maintained that only one thing solves every challenge in a commissioned sales business: keeping a robust, high-quality pipeline full of new prospects. Think about it. If you have 20 or 30 ideal prospects in your pipeline, and you have a methodology to continually refill that pipeline, you essentially have no difficult challenges in your sales business.

It became very clear that none of the five initiatives that this firm was chasing had anything to do with creating a robust pipeline or with holding high-quality open meetings with new clients. In reality, more than one of their highest objectives for the year actually hindered their ability to create a more robust sales climate. They had a key focus on sales closings but none on the front end of the sales cycle. Our single-minded focus became quite obvious: Hold five opens per advisor, per month, and track those results as the primary (ideally the only) single-minded focus for the entire organization.

What occurred immediately was the stark realization that all the advisors had limited pipelines, and more importantly, they had no effective strategies, designs, or tactics to fill their pipelines. It's hard to invite and hold meetings with prospects that do not exist.

We now had single-minded focus: Five open meetings per month, per advisor, would dramatically increase sales by design. As a next step, we had to begin to track results maniacally.

"What gets measured, gets managed," Peter Drucker declared. We were going to begin to measure and track.

WHAT THE HECK IS MANIACAL TRACKING?

Maniacal tracking, like single-minded focus, creates newfound learning and growth results simply by tracking more curiously, more aggressively, and more thoroughly than you or your team has done previously. For example, if you and your team want to move from 26 open meetings per year to 60, your tracking of those meetings will affect your results as much as simply conducting the meetings without much conscious tracking.

Go back to the cultural bias of "any client is a good client." Chances are, when you put into place the idea that if you hold 60 open meetings as opposed to 26 in a year, with a consistent 50 percent closing ratio, you will move from 13 new paying clients to 25—almost double—simply by focusing your efforts on one area of single-minded focus. Initially, the same challenges will take place, namely, financial advisors will track only the quantity, not the quality, of the clients. Sixty client meetings are way better than 26 in a year—or are they?

We allowed the firm to grow the new muscles associated with increasing the financial advisors' activities associated with filling their pipelines, holding more meetings, and in the first year, they actually grew sales by 178 percent! All of this, they realized, occurred mostly by focusing only on one objective, managing toward that objective, and maniacally tracking the results. They fell short of 60 new open meetings for the year but averaged 49—up significantly from 26 the year before.

Here is where the maniacal tracking started to help. In year two, they followed a growth year of 178 percent with a second year of 86 percent, again with the same single-minded focus. The odd thing, however, is that they did not raise the number of open meetings in year two. Their maniacal tracking led them to significantly increase the quality rather than quantity of their open meetings. The logic was pretty simple and counter to the cultural bias of any client being a good client. Instead, in addition to tracking the overall number of open meetings, they also tracked the number of meetings held with platinum, or ideal, clients—better-fitting and higher-revenue clients. If the revenue of a platinum client was two or three times that of a less attractive client, they could both grow their revenue exponentially and work fewer hours. This requirement of transformation tends to drive innovation and learning, combining the power of both single-minded focus and maniacal tracking.

Here are some of the items they tracked differently in year two:

- Does the client introduction come from a platinum or AAA client?

- How many introductions each year are classified as platinum, AAA, AA, or A type clients? (Note: A clients are no longer desired by this firm and present a bit of a dilemma.)

- At what point in our process do we refer out the A clients? The AA clients?

- Who among our current clients introduces us to the most new people? Why?

- How do we encourage and stimulate a natural process of introductions from our best-referring platinum and AAA clients but not from AA and A clients?

- How do we limit or filter introductions of AA and A clients? When these clients are referred, to whom do we then refer them?

- How do we create all of our services and products to attract and delight platinum clients?

You can imagine that once these sales advisors realized that every platinum client was worth two AAA clients and more than four AA clients, they began to track—maniacally—where the introduction came from, what demographics were involved, how suitable the clients were for the type of service the firm offered, and so on. Quantity took a back seat to quality, as doubling the quantity would have become impossible quite quickly.

Initially, increasing the number of open meetings from two to five per advisor took every bit of focus, creativity, effort, and attention they had to offer. Eventually, they realized as a team that if they only held two platinum open meetings every month, they could still dramatically increase sales *and do so by working much less!* My job as their coach was to demand innovation and transformation as part of their new focus and sales design. Imagine the natural sense of progress that each member of this firm enjoyed by engaging more clients at higher levels of sophistication and income, all the while working fewer hours. Their sales in two years more than tripled while taking on fewer clients and working less!

By the way, all this improvement required zero motivation. The leadership team could have used traditional incentives or bonuses or, from the other end of the spectrum, excruciating physical punishment, and neither form of motivation would have resulted in a result close to what they accomplished.

Needless to say, this firm continues to experience very high rates of growth and also refers out much business—the clients who no longer fit their model very well.

By designing and employing one single-minded focus and

then maniacally tracking results, you can dramatically shift your revenue results, your health, or any other important aspect of your life—all predictably and according to what matters most to you and your team!

CHAPTER 10

The Role of Self-Responsibility in Getting Great Results

WHEN CEOS AND team leaders complain that they don't know how to keep their team members motivated, I tend to want to puke on their shoes. Their job simply does not involve daily, weekly, monthly, or even worse, hourly motivation. When team leaders focus time on motivation, they are missing much more important opportunities to lead, inspire, and model for their team. Their unexamined thought process goes like this: "Since you are irresponsible or incapable of keeping your promises, I will motivate you daily to do so!"

In the end, who, then, is creating the problem—the CEO who keeps up this silly motivation game or the employee who continues to fall short of managing and fulfilling promises made? The answer tends to be "Yes!" since both parties are needed for this model to function.

When pushed, I always share with them the one core value that drives the most productive and effective teams: self-responsibility. Think about it. If all the members of your team arrive in a foul mood, hold limited or partial resources with which to fulfill their promises to the rest of the team, and are interrupted by a fire drill in the building, a foot of snow on the freeway, or the power going out, do they have a better chance of getting their work done in the face of these challenging circumstances if they possess a highly developed sense of self-responsibility or if they are highly motivated?

How about a well-coached athletic team in any sport? Do they win because they are highly motivated or because they perform their role on the team even when the weather is bad or adversity strikes in the game situation? I will take a less talented teammate that I can count on rather than an inconsistent performer who shows up fully only when motivated. I'll take the piss-poor-attitude team member who delivers as promised rather than the highly motivated sometimes performer any day of the week.

When team leaders get results out of their team (only) at

times of high motivation, there exists a dependency model that goes like this: "Give me proper motivation or an incentive to do great work, and I will do great work. If I do not feel properly motivated, the quality and volume of my work will decline in direct proportion to the decline in the amount of great motivation I receive."

That's why I want to puke on shoes when team leaders and CEOs try to focus on motivating their troops. Why not hire, instead, individuals who hold keeping their promises and self-responsibility among their highest values? Why not also encourage, acknowledge, and reward the simple, powerful value of self-responsibility? It solves way more problems, without much drama, than any high state of motivation ever will. Teach training and hiring self-responsibility, which looks and sounds like this in any team or organization: "If I can't keep a promise to a team or client, I manage the problem because I am self-responsible. I recommit, make a new promise with a clear deadline for completion, and communicate that to any and all stakeholders."

Imagine what challenges would simply disappear in your team or organization if all team members exercised a modicum of self-responsibility in their day-to-day fulfillment of promises internally and externally to your customers? Consider the astounding growth of Amazon as the predominant shopping site for almost anything. Amazon holds pretty simple principles: Deliver what we promise. Stand behind everything we sell. Refund without question if the customer is not happy. The emphasis on keeping delivery schedules and product quality promises, even though the company does not manufacture the vast majority of what it sells, keeps customers using the site as the quickest and most convenient choice for almost every product or service. The competitively fair prices and convenient delivery make the hassle of going to a store seem rather silly and wasteful.

HOW DO YOU FOSTER SELF-RESPONSIBILITY?

Earlier I mentioned that choosing or dictating an aspirational value, especially one spoken in a single word, falls flat with the team. Consider holding innovation as a core value for your organization. What does innovation mean to you? Now compare that to what innovation means to me, especially if we have to write our answers separately on a piece of paper. If you have 50 people in your organization, chances are very high that you will end up with 50 different versions of what innovation means.

Many organizations do this and with much inefficiency. Innovation is declared the highest or most cherished core value, and then the HR department has to educate and train

THE ROLE OF SELF-RESPONSIBILITY IN GETTING GREAT RESULTS

smaller teams to tease out and teach what exactly is meant by the term. The idea is that everyone will understand exactly what innovation means at your firm, and then they will all become much more capable of acting in a manner consistent with the teaching and training. First of all, what is the daily investment in taking an entire team out of production in order to train and teach them exactly what your team means by your one-word core value? All too often, I see teams make a focus out of one of the core values, and it becomes the subject of all the off-sites, training, and orientation classes. This approach is wasteful at best and highly inefficient at worst. Human beings can be taught the intended meaning of almost anything, but to the extent that they have their own distinctions, they will tend to live according to these distinctions much more than they will live according to what was taught to them.

Following are the two best ways to foster a strong sense of self-responsibility in your organization, in ranked order.

1. Hire people who hold as one of their highest personal core values the idea of keeping promises and completing tasks, even when big challenges appear, and recommitting when they fall short of their promised results. As simple as this sounds, no interview candidate has ever claimed to be a selfish player or a person who flakes on promises. Asking candidates if they hold

self-responsibility as a fundamentally high value will result in only one response: "Yes, I do!" Depending on your own company's hiring process, candidates can tell stories, give scenarios, or pass gauntlet, that demonstrate their consistent willingness and competence to produce results in spite of life's challenges. Anyone can produce with full resources, great teammates, and a great culture to work in. You want to find the people who have persevered and succeeded under less than ideal circumstances and when given only half of the needed resources. All of this can be teased out during the hiring process. Here are some suggested sample questions:

"What was the first (paid) job you held?" Look for people who developed young. Farm kids typify the attribute you want. If they do not feed the animals every day of the year, the animals die. Whether paid or not, this type of (self-)responsibility, when developed at a young age, plays well on teams. If the first job the candidate held was right out of college, chances are they have a less than developed need to create results without drama or excuses. Can they learn the ethic of self-responsibility? Sure, but it comes easier the earlier they had a responsibility to others in a team situation.

Another suggested question is to ask candidates

to "tell a story about getting disciplined or fired for not hitting objectives or promises. What were the circumstances, and what did you learn?" This one is more humbling, and you are cleverly looking to see if they can admit a time when they did not hit the mark. Every human being has missed deadlines, and candidates who can own the fact that they are not perfect, accept responsibility, and not blame others or other circumstances stand a much greater chance at success in your organization than those who have a story about how poor the working conditions were, what a lousy boss they had, or why they should have quit much earlier than they did. Who wants teammates like that—people who throw other people under the bus rather than work for a win for the team?

2. Create a directive for what self-responsibility (or any one-word value) means to your organization. The idea here is simple and works the way our brain works. When you ask any human being to be self-responsible, his or her interpretation or definition of what self-responsibility means will differ from yours and every other person's on the team.

Instead, consider telling them, or "directing" them,

what to do. Doing so will allow much less margin for misinterpretation. Much like a drill sergeant never asks but tells his troops what to do, a directive is heard much more clearly by our brains than is a request to be a certain way. Direct or command, and the team follows much closer and in unison. Given this concept, what might you command in order to ensure self-responsibility on your team? Consider these examples:

- Do what you promise. If impossible, recommit as early as possible.

- Complete what you commit to on time.

- Take initiative to finish what you start on time.

- Own your promises and complete them on time.

You could come up with several more that fit your organization or your team. The trick here is to nurture, encourage, acknowledge, and reward the organizational value that creates self-responsibility. A simple approach includes nominations by team members of other team members who exercised or demonstrated exceptional or noteworthy self-responsibility in the past week (they cannot nominate themselves). This could include working late to complete a project, solving a problem without prompting, or engaging a customer in creating a suitable solution to a mistake that our own team made.

When you direct or command your teammates to exercise self-responsibility regardless of their state of desire or motivation, they solve problems, create solutions, and complete a high degree of tasks on time and according to the promised conditions of satisfaction. In doing so, you significantly reduce the need to micromanage them or to meet with them to go over the status of projects. In this culture, leaders can lead more than they manage or troubleshoot. Team members can work more autonomously, and the culture developed in your organization can allow room for both professional growth and a significantly reduced reliance on drama or upset. Projects will flow much easier. People will coordinate much more fluidly. Promises will not always be kept, but this can always be managed. As a cornerstone core value, a directive that insists upon self-responsibility allows for adults to play together.

In contrast, children, regardless of the age on their driver's licenses, rely on excuses and circumstances. Nothing separates adults from children more in terms of maturity than does self-responsibility. If you are finding yourself managing and motivating people way too much, whether at home or in your team at work, chances are you have hired and nurtured a culture where children are allowed to give excuses instead of produce results. You want to raise children who become responsible adults. You want to work with people who say what they mean, do what they say, and do not expect a ribbon or trophy for fulfilling their simple promises.

Insist upon self-responsibility on your team, and some will leave rather than give up their right to complain, blame others, or give a great story as to why they could not possibly have produced an acceptable result on time. You will lose some talented people, but your culture will improve quite quickly because reliable and resourceful team members will remain. Imagine if everyone on the team needed full resources to complete promises on time. Wouldn't you succeed as a team more often if you employed self-responsible team members who exercised resourcefulness instead of missing a promised outcome or deadline?

Hire self-responsibility, and avoid most performance and attitude issues by design. This objective is simple and not terribly difficult to instill in your organization. Create your version of self-responsibility in the form of one simply stated directive, and then design hiring questions and tasks for the interview candidates to answer or complete. This will weed out those who simply do not believe in getting things done without excuses or motivation.

Building a strong organization starts first and foremost with a strong culture. A strong culture is built upon a foundation of simple, powerful core value directives that reveal and represent what you stand for as an organization. When self-responsibility sits as a foundational core value, your organization has gotten off to a very good start.

CHAPTER 11

Are You Running Toward or Away from Your Outcomes?

IT'S THE FINAL quarter of the year, and your team has a real chance to hit an all-time revenue goal. Everyone is on point. Everyone is pushing forward—maximum effort, full throttle, balls to the wall—all toward hitting a never-before-attained revenue number. Wow!

Are you running toward your best results ever, or are you running away from the possibility of the negative consequences that could result from not hitting your sales target? To your board members, this distinction may not matter one bit; their main concern will be that you hit the number. For your customers, one distinction will feel very different than the other; a team running full out toward a milestone goal makes for a much more enjoyable experience for the customers, the stakeholders, and of course, every member of your team. For those same customers, stakeholders, and team members, the feeling or experience associated with having to hit the goal or else does not hold the same enjoyable feeling. The customers feel pushed.

Here's the simple difference between the two scenarios, and it occurs in countless teams in the business world every day. At the midyear off-site, your stakeholders, your board of directors, and your immediate boss lay down the same mandate: Hit your sales target or risk a reduction in force! Clearly, this motivation is powerful, super clear, and unmistakable in its repercussions. Produce or risk unemployment not just for the sales team but for the entire organization. You and your sales team have all eyes on your production numbers, and, literally, your coworkers' jobs are at stake!

Alternatively, at that same midyear conference, those same stakeholders, your same board of directors, and your immediate boss all could set forth a robust plan to hit your all-time revenue goal, and in doing so, you, your team, and the entire organization then move to the next level of growth, profitability, expertise, and reputation. The entire team gets behind the initiative and takes ownership of the vision, the goal, the plan, and the eventual execution. Your team now starts the first day of the third quarter focused, energetic, and determined to work together to create an amazing result by year's end. The second half of the year will be very challenging and enjoyable indeed, and it will take a full team effort to succeed! You and your team readily accept the challenge set forth, with a bit of anxiety, yes, and also with confidence that you can do it.

Both sales scenarios are designed with the plan and outcome to create the exact same all-time revenue goal. Which scenario would you rather play in? Which scenario feels more like the team you play on?

The big difference rests on one simple, powerful notion: Is your team running toward (exactly) what you want or running away from the negative consequences of what you do *not* want?

Let's shift the scenarios to your personal fitness. After avoiding a trip to your cardiologist for years, despite chronic sluggishness, obesity, dangerously high cholesterol readings, and overall high blood pressure, you finally make the long overdue doctor's visit. Your doctor runs a full battery of tests and concludes that your health and longevity prospects do not look good should you continue on your current health path. Your immediate health risks can be dramatically lessened by a regimen that includes an improved diet and a weight loss of 30 pounds. Your trusted doctor insists that this dramatic outcome needs to be achieved in the coming 90 days.

Your doctor prescribes a routine that includes running at least 25 miles per week and a personal trainer who can help with the process of getting back into shape, losing the weight, and lowering your risks of a heart attack. Essentially, you have 90 days to hit your goal or else. Are you motivated to get moving? Will you show up at your workout tomorrow? I bet you will.

Now, with the same health circumstances described above, let's see if you recognize this situation from your team at work. One of your coworkers has a daughter with juvenile arthritis, and your teammate is inviting your entire organization to join him in running a half marathon or marathon to increase awareness about the effects of the disease and raise funds for research toward treatments and an eventual cure. You realize that you have at least 30 pounds to lose, and you think the world of your teammate. Against all athletic logic, and defying the odds of your ability to finish a long race, you sign up to run in the fund-raiser, which is scheduled in 90 days. You immediately feel anxious, excited, and proud, but then you ask yourself quietly, "What have I just done?"

You have committed to run farther than you have ever run, at perhaps the poorest state of personal fitness of your entire life, and there's no turning back. You have two objectives: get sponsors for your run and get in good enough shape to complete at least a half marathon. Since the run is only three months away, training must start first thing in the morning. Will you be there at the first workout? I bet you will.

Consider the two scenarios, both involving a process of getting up early to log miles, committing to a much healthier diet, taking off weight, and making progress very rapidly. With the juvenile arthritis scenario, every stride you make in your training is fueled by your sense of contribution and teamwork and colored boldly with the notion that if your teammate's daughter is tough enough to battle her disease, then you can train for and complete a half marathon. You push beyond physical and emotional barriers to stretch to your longest distance. You increase your total miles run every week. You work through blisters, soreness, and ankle pain to continue your training. You do all of this with a team of people from work, deepening your relationships with each person on your team. You run at lunch twice a week, in addition to your morning workouts. You also enjoy a sense of hero status from the other members of your organization who support the cause energetically, financially, and morally. Who knew that running could include so much benefit to you? Your team holds you in a newfound respect, both personally and professionally.

Finally race day arrives, and you feel ready to succeed. Last Saturday's long run was 10.5 miles, and today you will need to go 13.1 miles, an all-time personal record, to accomplish your half marathon goal. You have running partners, all who have become friends, running alongside. You have hit your individual and team fund-raising goal, all of which goes to research, and you have lost an amazing 31 pounds in the process. You look and feel better than you have in years, and none of your clothes fit properly due to the improved toning and weight loss. In short, every step you have taken on your journey has been in the direction of running toward *exactly what you wanted*. You chose a challenging goal, embraced the journey, and now are continuing to enjoy the process and the benefits. After the race, your entire team—pretty exhausted, quite pleased, and very celebratory—enjoys a post-race celebration.

You would do the whole thing over again in a heartbeat. At the post-race dinner, you commit to run again in next year's annual event. It now sounds like a lot of fun!

Alternatively, if you hit your same weight-loss goal mandated by the doctor, and monitored by a trainer, what fueled every step in your running process? My suggestion is that your entire process consisted of running away from an extremely negative outcome. How much fun is that, when you are putting in the same number of miles, probably by yourself or perhaps with only your trainer alongside? Every step is literally driven by fear—the fear of medical catastrophe or even death. Even in "success" you have to live in the shadow of "what if I backslide on my health or gain back ten pounds?" Do the negative consequences immediately reappear? Your clothes fit differently, you lost the needed 30 pounds, lowered your cholesterol and blood pressure numbers, and still, the lingering concern will not go away. You wonder if you have done enough.

As much as the physical rewards match in both scenarios, one feels dramatically different than the other. Same body. Same training. Same weight loss. Same improvement in looks. The difference is that the confidence and endorphins that accompany running toward your goals simply are not present in the running-away scenario.

In the end, fear-based motivation works very, very well, especially to drive short-term results. When Alec Baldwin in *Glengarry Glen Ross* outlined the top three sales prizes as a new Mercedes for first prize, steak knives for second prize, and losing your job for third prize, his team got into motion— really quickly. Activity increased, but did it improve? Most of the team crumbled under the stress. Fear works well but only to a point. Motivation, even positive motivation, emanates from *scarcity*, and scarcity equates directly with fear. Sadly, fear does work, and many team leaders resort to it to drive results, mostly because it works well for a while.

Conversely, other more evolved tools in your tool kit emanate from *abundance*, and abundance emanates from power. When your training regimen includes running with teammates, or your sales production numbers are founded on a base of power versus fear, or power versus force, your final results may not change much, but your experience associated with producing the successful results absolutely will. Power-based results are sustainable, and your team can build upon them. Force-based results rarely include the learning necessary to duplicate or innovate into the future.

THE ALGORITHM OF POWER VERSUS FORCE

In his seminal work, *Power vs. Force*, Dr. David Hawkins unveils an algorithm that calculates, among other things, the proportion of any population that lives life from a foundation of power, about one in seven, and the proportion that lives life from a foundation of force: six in seven. That is to say, only one in seven people at your work, in your community, or in our country lead, play, manage, or even live using a foundation of power or abundance. Not surprisingly, if six in seven live from a foundation of force or scarcity, it explains a lot of things, like surveys that confirm that 90 percent of drivers consider themselves "above average drivers." I suspect that when pushed, most of us would claim to live a life founded on power, despite the overwhelming odds against it. I know I do.

According to Hawkins, there exists only a one-in-seven chance that you or I live life from a base of power. What does this look like in practical terms? Let's give some simple examples. Living in power (or abundance) includes the notion of full self-responsibility versus blaming others. Living in power includes others by design versus excluding some. People who live from a base of power versus force manage much more wealth, and their power does not exist because they hold wealth. Quite the opposite. The wealth is created as *a direct result of* living from a foundation of power, which equates perfectly with abundance. People who live from a base of power share credit, take responsibility for mistakes, learn from them, and tend to express gratitude as a regular practice. Again, the gratitude is a prerequisite. The gratitude does not get expressed only when they feel as if they have received something worth expressing gratitude for.

Conversely, people who live from force keep score and frequently notice how they somehow get the short end of the proverbial stick. Forceful people often hold complaints and excuses. They literally attract things to complain about! Powerful people simply move forward, noting that circumstances have shifted, and life goes on. Imagine what living in either context might create when extracted over a lifetime! Our experience of everything from successes and failures to family relationships and blessings becomes colored dramatically by the simple choice to live in power (abundance) or force (scarcity).

If the choice to live from a position of power exists as just that—a choice—then what is power, and how can it be distinguished? As I said earlier, *power equals a position, stance, or move that generates no counter.* Does that make power strategic? Sure, but power is not based in great strategy. Instead, power is based in love. Consider that a powerful move engages people, unites people, and gets people into action—without the need for unnecessary politics, complaining, or division. Does your team leader engage you in loving your role, loving your team, and loving your work? Successful leaders do this well and naturally. Again, statistically, only one in seven leads from a base of power, abundance, and love. In the end, all three attributes essentially create the same results.

Conversely, *force equals an exercise in a necessary amount of dominance in order to create a result.* Recall the "hit your sales goal or lose your job" scenario, or your doctor warning that you either lose 30 pounds in 90 days or risk catastrophic results. Both scenarios require a necessary amount of force to get you moving. You are dominated or pushed into a direction or decision that you feel you have little or no choice in creating. You would not otherwise choose this direction or objective. You are partially or fully forced to create an outcome you have not fully bought into.

Force requires justification and often attracts dissension and pushback. Sadly, force also tends to silence and perturb those same dissenters rather than engage them in strengthening the position, the argument, and the momentum in a positive direction. Force moves us, at times, against our will or better judgment. Power invites us to move forward of our own choosing, with clarity and resolve.

In the end, engaging power versus force engages the brain differently. Ever notice that when an idea is your own, you act on it naturally, and when the idea (or decision) is dictated, you naturally have questions, need clarification, and find holes in the decision? Your brain simply does not support decisions thrust upon you, and as such, the results tend to fall short of those when all voices—especially your own—are heard.

Ultimately, motivation exists as a function of force, even when the motivation creates a very positive tit-for-tat equation. Utilizing tools that allow every person on your team to play of their own accord engages talent, emotion, and ownership that needs no additional or constant attention. Power creates this dynamic.

I invite you to choose a powerful platform as one of your most effective tools. Statistically, you will be a long shot, and your team members will love you for that!

CHAPTER 12

The Incredible Power
of Scenario Building

IN THE EARLY 1970s, the United States experienced the first
of two devastating OPEC-driven energy crises. OPEC cut oil
supplies by design, and gas shortages ensued, which included
rationing and two-hour waits to purchase fuel at inflated
prices. The lifeblood of our economy—namely cheap, subsidized oil—doubled in price and crippled our economy, sinking
the country into a deep recession.

One oil company, Royal Dutch Shell, seemed to thrive much
better than its rivals in the United States. Why? The answer
now seems very simple: Royal Dutch Shell had engaged in a
proactive process of scenario building well in advance of the
oil shortages, such that when the crisis hit, Shell Oil was much

better prepared to take effective actions. Hence, the leaders had already gone through the planning and thought processes required to move more quickly. They created clarity for their employees and customers and remained profitable when the rest of the industry reeled.

WHAT IS SCENARIO BUILDING?

Scenario building represents a simple, powerful tool that simply allows us to ask, "What if?" without the necessity to commit to any firm course of action. Stronger than a BS session, or even a whiteboard meeting, scenario building allows anyone— you, me, or us together—to engage in a substantive discussion where we harvest possibilities that simply did not exist before and that are ideally connected to our Highest Purpose or Why.

Especially effective if you are not yet (fully) living out your Highest Purpose or Why, scenario building requires that we float a possibility previously considered even outlandish and then slowly create it and build it out into a possible reality.

In the late 1960s, Royal Dutch Shell employed the same oil strategy as Exxon, Chevron, and Standard Oil. The American oil companies extracted oil from Middle Eastern companies, shared some revenues with the countries of origin, and then exported that heavily subsidized oil back to the United States for refining into gasoline for our booming auto-driven economy. The oil came essentially free (or at least, at a very low cost) as long as the host countries stayed happy. The host countries, for their part, did not have the equipment or expertise to find and extract the oil, so the partnership made great sense—until it no longer did.

Eventually, the host countries, organized into what we now call OPEC, the Organization of the Petroleum Exporting Countries, nationalized the oil fields, essentially telling the US companies that they, the host companies, would now control the production of all oil in their home countries. By limiting the supply, the members of OPEC could drive prices much higher and make more money by pumping a lot less oil—a simple case of supply and demand.

Supplies indeed shrunk, almost overnight, and chaos in the US economy ensued. The problem was pretty simple. The United States did not own the underlying mineral rights, nor did they own the land under which the oil reserves existed. The host countries did not care much that the US companies owned the equipment used to extract the oil. The home countries claimed that equipment as their own, since it was used on their land.

It now seems incredible that none of the US oil companies were prepared for such a simple shift—that the host countries would take back control of production in their own countries—but none, except for Shell Oil, planned for such an event.

Shell gathered leadership teams in advance of a perceived (risky) scenario and asked, "What if this were to occur?" Did they plan for the nationalization of the oil fields in the OPEC member countries? Perhaps they worked on that exact scenario. Chances are they held scenarios that resulted in the same outcome, namely, the cutoff of the supply of cheap oil to the United States. Shell Oil was much better prepared than its counterparts not only to survive but to thrive in the face of chaos.

HOW CAN I MAKE SCENARIO BUILDING WORK FOR MY TEAM?

Scenario building now exists in the form of whiteboard sessions, innovation, creativity labs, and many other forms. Done well, scenario building creates new companies, new ideas, and newly possible results, seemingly out of thin air. More importantly, scenario building done well engages teams and individuals to do the best work of their lives. Here are some fundamental keys to successful scenario building:

Start with "What if?" The phrase *what if* engages our brain in a specific fashion so as to encourage creativity, curiosity, and no firm commitment, all at the same time. The energetic combination of creativity and curiosity creates a powerful foundation upon which to engage team members in an idea or notion that was heretofore considered unthinkable or inconceivable. When you use the phrase, you are acknowledging that the outcome you propose is outside of what now seems reasonable, and you are not committing to it. If not used by design, the language would simply sound more like this: "How do we get to $10 million this year?" The word *how* implies that the decision has already been made and that the result is merely a matter of figuring out who does what and how quickly in terms of strategies, tactics, and execution. It is also much more confronting than *what if,* which implies that we are inventing, designing, and creating—but also not committing just yet.

Step 1: Engage your team in a possibility.

Develop a clear scenario—Our brains are wired to focus on specifics, such as numbers, visuals, great stories, and clear outcomes. The clearer and more compelling the what-if scenario, the more successful your team will be in creating buy-in, engagement, and, eventually, full ownership of your scenario. If you want confusion and lack of agreement, try scenarios expressed as themes or trends. These make for murky scenarios since our brains only hear what we want to hear within the trend or theme. Consider these two scenarios:

"What if our team had its best year ever?"

"What if our team hit the $10 million gross revenue mark this year?"

Does one scenario equal or include the other? I suspect that if your team hit the $10 million mark, it would, by definition, equal the best year ever in terms of sales. Your brain would need to wrap around the idea of hitting an ambitious sales number, and all the supporting projects needed in order to accomplish this would simply start happening. All supporting projects would fall in line with the overriding, uncomplicated outcome: Hit the $10 million sales mark. Would you need an improved or additional product? Would your delivery and fulfillment approach have to change? Could your team handle the production level with their current members, or is there a key hire or two that would need to take place? How soon would you need these additional team members in order to accomplish your objective? Any and all projects required to hit the $10 million mark would show up in context.

The questions would all come quickly, specifically because your scenario would engage the brain in one function: hitting the $10 million sales mark. You would only increase staffing in pursuit of your single goal. You would redesign or improve the product line in order to increase sales. You would travel more (or less) in order to succeed in your objective. The $10 million production level would focus your brain on one main objective and create the condition of satisfaction for the entire team. My brain would end up on the same focus as yours, even if we held very different roles in the organization. We could even disagree on how to get to our new sales number, specifically because we have already agreed on hitting it.

With the first scenario, your brain naturally goes to your version of our "best year ever," and my brain goes to my version, and my version is probably very different than yours. Thematically, having our best year ever seems like a worthwhile endeavor. The differences in versions show up pretty quickly, however, diluting focus and dividing ownership. Specifically, my version might include increased sales, yes, and perhaps a promotion for me (but maybe not for you), less travel, a new full-time assistant, and a full redesign of the product line. Would these objectives be included in your version of our best year ever? Your version may or may not include any of my ideas, and hence, the whiteboard session would have an almost unlimited amount of ideas, making the end product much more difficult to agree upon or act upon. In the end, your best ideas or my best ideas—at least some of them—would not make the cut, so both of us would feel slighted. Buy-in would be compromised somewhat, as I fought for my version of our best year ever according to my agenda, and you fought for your version, and all the other team members fought for their versions, all of which would be rooted in the thematic rather than specific wording of the scenario.

Step 2: Get specific.

Articulate singular, simple scenarios—In order to solve problems, there is only one key: Solve one challenge or problem at a time. If your team members are late for work, and their focus is lacking, you have two challenges to solve, not one. Solve them individually rather than together. Will focus improve if teammates all show up on time? Maybe. Will punctuality improve if focus improves? Again, perhaps. However, it is much simpler to solve the two challenges separately. Solve one after another, or even two at the same time, but only after you separate the challenges in order to solve them quicker. The same rule applies with successful scenario building. An economy of words (simplicity) and a singular focus (clarity) produce the necessary power to design successful outcomes.

"What if our team hits the $10 million gross sales mark this year?"

Simple? Yes. Singular challenge? Yes. Will it create one conversation rather than multiple conversations? Yes. This one key criterion works wonders to find out if your what-if scenario has the possibility of creating what you want: clear focus, full engagement, all voices heard, and, in the end, full ownership from the team.

Step 3: Articulate simple, clear, singular scenarios.

Stay in charge rather than in control—You've likely been in a meeting where the team leader is editing "good ideas" from "bad ideas," in essence driving one point of view. Only the leader's ideas make the whiteboard. This type of meeting is very frustrating for the participants, especially when the clear invitation was to "float lots of new ideas."

If you are a team leader running the meeting, choose your role: Either be in charge or be in control. The difference is profound and will dictate how robust your scenario ends up.

Being *in control* usually looks like you have a limited array of possibilities that you are willing to entertain, and anything else gets deleted, altered, censored, tabled, or stonewalled. Consider the effects of any of those actions on the participants in that meeting. They were asked to participate in a whiteboard session to come up with goals and objectives for next year, but the hidden and unannounced rule continues to appear: Only ideas advanced by the senior leadership team, the sales team, the product team, or the team leader will be entertained. The question then seems only fair: "Why did you invite me to participate if the options have already been created?" The unwritten rule surfaces rather quickly that the "ideas" are really an excuse to begin a process of buy-in from team members—buy-in of ideas they never created or signed off on.

When you are *in charge of* the discussion, you make sure

that all voices, all ideas, and all possibilities are floated, and this is easier to say than it is to accomplish. Here is a simple tool to help with that process. Try it at every meeting, and tie it to the purpose of the meeting. If you want to solicit and elicit new ideas, ask your participants how they need to be or what is necessary to accomplish the objective at hand. If you are in a decision-making meeting, the list you come up with will look radically different from the list associated with an ideation meeting. In the end, each person present makes one contribution, without duplication, until every participant has given as many suggestions as they would like. Generally, it takes two turns around the room to capture all suggestions on how participants need to be to accomplish the intended result of the meeting. For an ideation or whiteboard session, here is what your list might include, all voiced by your participants:

- suspension of judgment

- curiosity

- playfulness

- no sarcasm (it kills ideas)

- courage

- no limits or boundaries

- full respect for all ideas

- confidentiality (not always needed)

- teamwork

- collaboration

- creativity

The list will most likely have twelve to fifteen items on it, and the key is to solicit this from the participants rather than providing the list yourself. Once the list has been created, ask one question in order to cross off any superfluous items from the list: "If we engaged in this way of being, would the conversation be unsafe?" For almost all items on your list, the answer will be no, and the suggestion will stay. Any suggestions that could create an unsafe space come off the list. One such item might be "consensus," which could be considered unsafe because of the pressure to go along with an idea rather than oppose it. This pressure limits input and, thus, would make the space unsafe.

Once you have checked each suggestion for safety, ask each participant to agree by the raising of hands (not a voice vote) that they each agree to abide by these "Common Grounds" during your meeting. You avoid a voice vote because some may not say anything, and that gives them a secret out on behaving as you all just agreed. You can see hands raised, and you can more easily confirm agreement with the proposed Common Grounds.

You have now set the room up as a safe space in which to ideate as a group. You are now in charge. As the leader in charge (or if you are simply facilitating the meeting), *any and all ideas are now possible and welcome.* You capture them, acknowledge the speaker of the idea (very important in order to engage all voices), and follow up with a "veto vote" if you need it after the meeting has concluded, since you do not have to decide anything today. An ideation meeting creates proposals, none of which have to be adopted in the same meeting.

By leading the meeting from the position of being in charge, you have set the stage to engage and hear all voices, and the ideas are those of the team versus your own or those of a faction or clique. You may be pleasantly surprised to hear that the team considers possibilities that you (or the leadership team) had not previously thought of.

You are as human as anyone. When the idea is your own, you like it, and you naturally take action toward achieving it. The same rule holds true when the team creates an idea in real time—everyone hears it, everyone has a voice to help develop it, and in the end, everyone owns the idea and the outcome as their own creation. Your job as the team leader gets much easier by being in charge rather than attempting to control the outcome.

Step 4: Stay in charge and allow the team to create the outcome that your entire team owns.

Solicit and engage all voices—This final step is critical and requires two methods of accomplishing the task at hand.

If every member of the meeting has spoken, given input, and actively participated in the discussion, great! Your job of being in charge has been made very easy indeed. Your job is to take note that every person has offered input, ideas, and critical feedback or has asked questions. If not, here is the simple second way to accomplish this: Break your big group into three-person teams and give each team a part of the scenario you are building to discuss and then report back to the whole group. For example, if you are debating the correct revenue figure to go after, have one team discuss and "advise" the whole group on the merits of $10 million versus a higher or lower figure. Have another group discuss and make recommendations on other aspects of the scenario, such as what projects, in priority order, should the team take on first in order to hit the record sales number.

Remember, none of these recommendations have to be correct, nor do they have to be agreed upon. You are simply raising the odds that all voices contribute to (and hence, own) the final proposal adopted.

Step 5: Engage all voices, on purpose!

Check to see if our values are aligned and fully engaged by the scenario—The last step is quite simple and easy. Assuming that you have clearly articulated values and directives for your organization, ask this question: Will pursuing our proposed (remember, it's still a proposal until adopted) scenario require us to become more of our best, or will it detract from our doing great work?

As long as engaging in the pursuit of the scenario requires you to live out your Highest Purpose, your Why, and requires you to do the best work of your life, then you have built a tremendously powerful scenario. Go and crush it!

Step 6: Quality-check your scenario.

Scenario building allows you to float a possibility that connects you and your team to a vehicle much more powerful than motivation—namely, your Highest Purpose, or Why. That purpose, or Why, becomes the incredibly strong driver for your end results, as you are fueling your activities connected to your highest values rather than centering on the process or the work associated with accomplishing a goal. You and your team will naturally want to play and will run toward the scenario that you build together.

Consider what might happen in your team or family if you lived from a clearly articulated Highest Purpose, or Why.

Go find out!

CHAPTER 13

Your Secret Weapon

EVER VOLUNTEER AT a homeless shelter, a Habitat for Humanity work site, or a kids' charitable event? You sign up and go with the idea that you will "bless" others, and at the end of your shift, your long day, or the final celebratory meal, you feel as though you have received more in the way of blessings than any one person or group of people whom you intended to bless. Why is this so?

It's pretty simple. There exists a point in life where service stands as a calling all by itself. When you serve, you give for the sake of giving. The energy created in a group improves, and the people who surround you tend to model your service mentality. Defined roles become less important. No job is beneath anyone, especially you. You are simply engaging a powerful secret weapon: service. Much like the energy that surrounds the giving of a gift with no expectation of a return gift, you benefit from the feeling of doing something worthy.

We have all received a gift that was presented as such but quickly showed itself to have strings attached. Service never shows up in this light. You give or serve as an offering or a gift to others rather than for what you can receive in return.

One of my earliest clients became an advisor to me, and I asked him if he could share the most beneficial lesson he had learned in his long legal career. Stan enjoyed a well-earned reputation as a legendary attorney who created many of the most utilized strategies to stay ahead of the tax law changes that would come every year. His law partner was more famous because he would speak at conventions and present (and then sell) these ready-made solutions to financial planners. Stan was the proverbial steak, and his partner was almost all sizzle. They made for a robust partnership.

Stan's advice came in the form of a story. He married in the 1950s while in his last year of law school. His wife, Muriel, was the youngest of four daughters and from a prominent family. Shortly after he and Muriel were married, they happily found out that they were expecting. His father-in-law had a tradition with each of the other three sisters, all of whom were married, that he would present or "gift" a check in the amount of $10,000 each year. For context, Stan was hoping for a starting salary after law school of $12,000, so the gift was quite substantial.

Stan had the advantage of being around the family while dating Muriel, and he noticed that his future in-laws acted in a way that at times gave them power over their daughters and over their sons-in-law by default. One of the couples was advised against purchasing their first home, by the in-laws, of course, and since the down payment money for the home came from them, the advice certainly had to be heard. It was never spoken, but it made sense to accept and follow the advice.

The most powerful lesson that Stan shared with me was that he politely declined the first check from his in-laws, having decided that he wanted to create a family with his wife without oversight from anyone else. His declination was taken with public grace by his father-in-law. Privately, his father-in-law and Stan both acknowledged that Stan would earn his own way in the world, and had he accepted the gift, he and Muriel would also have had to accept and adhere to unsolicited guidance as well. The lesson learned: Only engage clients, family, or friends whose gifts or service comes without strings attached; otherwise, be prepared to accept some measure of retribution.

With your team, with a charity, or with your family, when you work in the spirit of service rather than with strings attached, you and those whom you serve both benefit and tend to thrive. And when the day is done, you feel blessed and used up for the people and purpose you support. Your contribution stands simply, beautifully, fully intended, fully given. Key to the ethic and spirit of service is the idea that it is freely given, without anything expected in return. The blessing then becomes yours despite the sweat, the challenges, the calluses, and the fatigue. Your service mirrors the energy in giving a gift without expectation for something in return. In the end, the giving becomes your contribution and also your blessing to receive. This creates the real power in serving others.

In the same way, donating money to a worthy cause creates a feeling you cannot replicate by purchasing any type of consumer good—even if that consumer good holds status, sex appeal, or panache of some sort. Consider buying an outfit that makes you look great and suits you perfectly—fits well, is the perfect color, and is sexy. You willingly purchase the outfit and feel great wearing it. The expenditure of money might come along with a sense of indulgence, pride, or guilt, especially if financed on a credit card.

Now compare the feeling you get from writing a check or donating a day of service to a cause you really believe in. Perhaps your nieces or nephews are selling holiday wrapping paper to support their school, or you are sponsoring a child in a developing country. You may have worked a day or a week at a Habitat for Humanity project, despite having little or no carpentry skills. It might be a political or humanitarian cause.

The key is that you strongly believe in the cause—to the point where you are willing to write a check or donate your time in service.

You do so out of a sense of love, a connection to what matters most to you, not out of pleasure. Hence, the feeling created is different in your brain's hierarchy of feelings and power. Love versus craving. Love versus ego. Love versus indulgence. Service and love reside in the same zip code. That's why your contribution of service to others on your team, in your family, or in your community mirrors that feeling you get when writing a check to an organization or person you strongly believe in.

The check written to a cause you believe in creates a sense of service much like the feeling created when you serve your team and its members. Either way, you work, and you may even work harder when you do it from a place of service rather than from fulfilling your role at a high level. The difference is sustainability. You can sustain a pace built on a foundation of service, whereas motivating or driving people requires increasingly more motivation or more drive going forward. It becomes the ultimate dependency model.

Ask yourself, "If I felt as though I was serving those I love and care about every day, would I need to get motivated to do it, or would I simply show up ready to go?" Service provides this sustainable, very powerful leadership platform—a platform not reachable through the use of motivation.

CAN YOU SIMPLY CHOOSE SERVICE AS A CONTEXT?

We have all given a gift or served at a charity that matters to us. The powerful benefit we receive in return feels like this: When you plan, shop for, wrap, and then present a gift to a cherished friend or family member, don't you enjoy the entire process? When they say, "I love it! Thank you so much!" isn't your reply something like this? "I'm so glad you like it. It was really fun to pick out!"

If service holds the similarly powerful state of energy as giving a gift, consider that service as a leadership platform begins at the same point: care or love. Leaders who really care about their team members, rather than caring about driving those team members to produce revenue or results, ironically tend to produce much better overall results. If service as a "strategy" works so well as a leadership platform, can you simply "choose" to serve and then enjoy the benefits in terms of personal satisfaction, higher engagement from team members, the building of a closer-knit community, and a high-performing team?

Don't we all wish it were so easy! As with many things in life, simple does not equal easy. Logically, all team leaders, parents, coaches, and teachers should simply shift their operating context to a service mode, and better results and happier team members will follow. The problem is, when service, like gift giving, is used as a tactic, it does not produce those results. Team members, like recipients of gifts with strings attached,

quickly sense the tactic and become cautious. If you're thinking that you'll adopt service as your highest core value, it's
most likely that you will have a mess to clean up.

Just as declaring yourself a world-class athlete does not give
you a single-digit body fat percentage and superior cardiovas-
cular and muscular performance, neither does "choosing" service as the highest state of performance suddenly turn you into
a service-oriented player. Nor does it make your teammates
willing to recognize and accept your gift and operating mode
of service.

You will have to work yourself up to the point where your
team embodies and models your service, and, simultaneously,
your service mentality is unshakable and unmistakable. Over
a very short period of time, individuals and groups of people
will recognize that what you do far outweighs what you *say*
you will do—either you lead from a sense of purpose, a sense
of service, or a sense of contribution, or you do not. Your fate
is then sealed to a certain extent.

Clicking into service mode fools no one, and when leaders suddenly attempt to adopt a service mentality, the attempt
comes off as a poorly masked and much less powerful state of
being. The tactic falls flat and creates an assessment of the team
leader as manipulative rather than powerful. Your team will
most likely interpret the shift to service as a scheme, tactic, or
tit-for-tat approach where they would have to respond in kind

to your service offerings. In the end, the manipulation shows up as a shady form of motivation and almost always backfires.

In contrast, when leaders consistently serve their team members, their board, and their customers as their primary operating mode, they can still employ other tactics, strategically and for a short period of time, without disregarding their well-earned reputation and primary service operating mode. In short, their teammates trust that the service mode will return right after the quarter closes, the short-term push is over, or the performance reviews are completed. It does not lessen a leader's power to serve, nor does it exempt the leader from having to make difficult decisions, let staff go, or cut budgets. Service simply stands as the regular operating mode for some powerful leaders, and they can utilize other tools when necessary.

Try this exercise in your next hiring interview. Ask the candidate to list whom they currently serve. If they look at you with an odd sense of confusion, they have answered quite clearly that service is not a regular operating mode for them. There is no reason to dismiss them as a candidate, but do not expect them to live up to an authentically natural sense of service toward their teammates and customers.

If they answer affirmatively and offer a list, it might include God, their family, their children, the local Little League Association—the list could be quite large. Those who serve others understand and identify with the ethic of service. If your candidate has not served others in any capacity, you will know quite clearly, as this question is rarely in sample interview "prep" questions, so they will not be able to fake an answer very well.

Regardless of the cause they serve, the fact that they live their life in service to others makes them a potentially fabulous candidate for your team. We have found that 1 in about 30 people you might hire passes this simple gauntlet question.

As a secret weapon, authentically engaged service multiplies team performance, improves morale, and creates a culture where teammates desire to stay on any team you run—whether you are the CEO, a team leader, or the head of your family. Ever notice that when successful team leaders and managers move to a new position in a different firm, many of their former teammates reach out to see if they can be brought on as well? This phenomenon rarely happens with team leaders who push, pull, or motivate to create results.

I often ask a simple, piercing question of my coaching clients when they engage in habits, behaviors, or relationships that harm them or appear as toxic. "How does that behavior (or relationship) serve you?" Without fail, every client says the exact same thing in response: "It doesn't." The fact is, if you routinely stay up too late or drink too much or hang out with the wrong crowd, it actually does serve you. If not, you would gladly and quite logically choose another course of action. Service always creates an outcome that we desire. When leaders "serve" in order to drive results, chances are they will create unintended dysfunction. When leaders serve out of a natural sense of giving a gift of themselves, they also create outcomes, but those outcomes usually are much more beneficial and, ironically, profitable and productive.

Whom do you serve, and more importantly, why? If you realize that you really serve only yourself, ask yourself this question: "If I could serve anyone, who would it be?" When you adopt this attitude and mentality to serve others, your results and your energy dramatically increase as you perform on purpose rather than at gunpoint.

This should begin to propel you in the right direction!

———

Moving Forward

REGARDLESS OF WHETHER you run a business, manage a family, or participate in a favorite club, having your team succeed, thrive, and grow really affects your enjoyment, not to mention your wallet and your psyche. You may as well enjoy the process and succeed, as you're going to put the time in anyway. Succeeding often depends on the path you take and the tools you choose to employ on your way to the success you desire.

If you still want to employ motivation all of the time, I commend your energy and stick-to-itiveness. Motivation may end up getting you where you want to go. It may also wear you out. In the end, when employing motivation, you are entering an ongoing contract that goes like this: "Every time you do not feel like doing what you have committed to, I will step in and help you to derive enough energy or desire to keep going . . . until such time as you require yet another boost."

As my original partner told me right from the get-go: "Motivation is exhausting! There is no way we will motivate anyone." My partner was right. Once you take on the task of incentives, tit-for-tat deals, or constant monitoring of results, you have shifted your actual role from team leader to team babysitter. Get ready for exhaustion and frustration. To those CEOs who motivate as your highest role, again, get ready for long hours, performance tied to your ability to motivate daily, and energy-dependent team members.

In the end, every company desires team members who show up ready to produce results, do so with skill and a good attitude, and contribute to their teammates and the customers your team serves. Anything short of that means that you and your leadership team are engaging in dependency tools. Don't look for the team members to shift. You will need to shift first.

Are you skilled with systems? How well do you design or implement processes that ensure reliable results? Combine either of these tools with a dash of motivation, and your path in life will become much easier, not to mention more predictable. You were kind of built this way, so if the horse is going in that direction, far better to go with it than attempt to force the horse (or the herd!) to move in a direction they have no desire to go.

Do you inspire naturally? Lead from whatever role you hold? Find the purpose for activities you participate in? Do you serve your team and your customers? Do so from your heart, and your team will respond in kind.

Again, when you combine your natural abilities in leadership, inspiration, and creating purpose with just a touch of motivation, watch how much your results multiply when compared with attempting to motivate at every turn. In the end, a pilot light that never goes out acts much like purpose, rather than trying to cook everything on high heat, as you have to do with motivation. In the end, you can always add more heat with a constantly burning pilot light, but turning down the heat after a dish has been scorched or burned does not work so well. Much like heat, motivation should always be used in small doses and turned up only for short periods of time.

Purpose, service, love, systems, processes, directives, habits—pick your tools. In the end, chopping down a tree using a sixteen-pound sledgehammer will take a very long time and require much more effort than would utilizing a more appropriate tool, like a bow saw or an axe.

Go forth and strive, grow, learn, and, mostly, succeed! And for goodness' sake, stop motivating!

Acknowledgments

SOME PEOPLE ACTUALLY read the acknowledgments section, and evidently, this includes you.

Friends and associates have asked me for years to write a book—just not this one, but another topic, which I declined. Their rationale went like this: Writing a book is "the new business card" and gives you much more visibility and credibility. That rationale made me want to vomit . . . onto my own shoes.

A trusted friend and conspirator, Christina Harbridge, then connected me to the reason to write—that it might help someone—and I started writing the next day. Christina knew that the reason to write made all the difference, and my intentions to do almost anything are normally built on partnering with people to create a big win. My sincere thanks, Christina, for your wisdom, counsel, and mostly, your friendship. This book simply would not exist without your contributions during several stages in the process.

Simon Sinek, another friend and collaborator, really helped at the right time with just the right guidance and counsel.

Simon's input helped to keep me on track—about writing and blocking out the outside noise. ADHD had not been discovered when I was a kid, or else I would have been the poster child for that affliction. Writing and ADHD do not make great partners. Simon helped to keep me on target to finish what I started and, more importantly, to do what I love. He continues to connect me and others to their Why, and it continues to make a difference.

Paul Leboffe, a friend and the brother I never had, nurtured and encouraged me throughout several points in this writing process. Paul has always been a pansophic artist, Renaissance man, and gifted coach, and he continues to pour into me in countless ways. Paul and I have also worked as partners and continue to collaborate in all kinds of ways. Without Paul's encouragement, at best this book would have taken twice as long to write.

To my confidential friends and conspirators of MOTH (Men Of The House), a nonexistent mastermind that meets in secret, my mythical associates encouraged and supported the idea of a book. Thank you for your support and mandates to keep going.

The team at Greenleaf has been great to work with, at every step of the way. Starting with Jay, who flat out lied to me (at my specific request) about fictitious deadlines and in doing so helped me to move quickly, to Justin, Stephanie, Tyler, Kristine,

Christine, and Carrie. Those are just the people I remember, and the entire team has been both fun and productive to work with, especially since I was a rank amateur in the process of writing and publishing a book.

Finally, my wife, Radhika, aka "Beans," has played an important dual role. She has been steadfastly and enthusiastically encouraging as well as super patient in *not* reading the manuscript. Given my shyness about sharing a "work in progress," she kept urging me to make progress at every point and refrained from the spousal insistence to read the manuscript. Not surprising why she and I are such great partners.

To you, the enthusiastic reader, thank you for reading, learning, and growing from *The Motivation Trap*. I encourage you to find your voice and your most authentic way to lead and manage your team, your company, and your family. In doing so, you will create leaders long after you move on from your current role.

All the best!

About the Author

JOHN HITTLER is the cofounder of Evoking Genius, a transformational business-coaching firm based in San Jose, California.

Father of seven, happily married, competitive athlete, and dedicated volunteer in the field of domestic violence, John spends his free time dancing tango with his wife, cooking for his friends and family, and traveling to places he has not yet visited.

John can be reached at www.evokinggenius.com.